Parents in Prison: Addressing the Needs of Families

James Boudouris, Ph.D.

1996 Edition

Acknowledgments

I would like to thank the American Correctional Association for the opportunity to prepare the second edition of this book. The many individuals who supplied the information included in this survey were very kind to respond to our requests for information about their institutions and programs.

Special thanks to the individuals who provided photos: Penny Lucero, Assistant Warden, New Mexico Women's Correctional Facility, Grants, New Mexico and Angela Blom, Assistant to the Warden, Pocatello Women's Correctional Center, Pocatello, Idaho.

ACA Staff:
Bobbie L. Huskey, President
James A. Gondles, Jr., Executive Director
Gabriella M. Daley, Director, Communications and Publications
Leslie A. Maxam, Assistant Director, Communications and Publications
Alice Fins, Managing Editor
Michael Kelly, Associate Editor
Mike Selby, Production Editor

Cover photo by Grace Wojda. Used with permission of the photographer from *Women Behind Bars: A Photo Essay*, American Correctional Association, 1996.
Cover art by Graphic Mac, Washington, D.C.
Production by Violette Graphics, Gaithersburg, MD
Printed in the U. S. A. by Braceland, Philadelphia, PA

This publication may be ordered from:
American Correctional Association
4380 Forbes Blvd.
Lanham, MD 20706-4322
1-800-ACA-JOIN

Library of Congress Cataloging in Publication Data
Boudouris, James.
Parents in Prison: addressing the needs of Families/James Boudouris.
p. cm.
Rev. ed. of: Prisons and Kids. c1985.
"Second edition"—Ack.
ISBN 1-56991-050-2 (pbk).
1. Children of women prisoners—Services for—United States. 2. Children of women of prisoners—Services for—Canada. 3. Women prisoners—United States—Family relationships. 4. Women prisoners—Canada—Family relationships. 5. Prisoners' families—United States. 6. Prisoners' families—Canada. I. Boudouris, James. Prisons and kids. II. Title.
HV8886.U5B68 1996
362.7—dc20.

Contents

Foreword by James A. Gondles, Jr. v

Introduction vi

1. Parental Ties 1
- Bonding 1
- The Father's Role 6

2. Programs 11
- Problems with Facilities 11
- Recidivism Reduction 11
- Prison Nurseries 12
- Foreign Programs 13
- North American Experiences 16
- Children's Centers and Day Care Centers 21
- MATCH and PATCH Programs 21
- Parenting Classes. 24
- Child Rearing Attitudes of Incarcerated Parents 27
- Parenting Programs at Boot Camps 27
- Furloughs 28
- Family and Conjugal Visits 30
- Latin America 32
- Conjugal Visits in the United States 33
- The Debate on Conjugal Visits 33
- Community Facilities 34
- Visitation Policies 36
- Support Services 40
- Penal Colonies 43
- A Variety of Advantages 44
- Summary Discussion of Programs 45
- Family Advocacy 46

3. Legal Issues 53
- Class Action Suits 53
- Best Interests of the Child 55
- Permanency Planning 56
- Medical Care 59
- Liability 62

4. Administration 63
- Private Sector Corrections 63
- Planning and Program Development 63
- Recommendations 67

5. Table: 71
Institutional Programs for Incarcerated Mothers and Their Children 71

6. Policies 83
American Correctional Association: Public Correctional Policy on Female Offender Services - 1995 83
Federal Bureau of Prison's Policy Statement: Parenting Program Standard - 1995 84
Uniform Law Commissioners' Model Sentencing and Corrections Act - 1979 87

7. References 89

8. Resources 97
Contacts 97
Community Programs and Resources 104

Foreword

We appreciate the efforts of James Boudouris, Ph.D. in compiling this volume. Since his work of more than ten years ago in *Prisons and Kids*, he has updated his findings and research. More than seventy-four state prisons, nine federal facilities, and three Canadian prisons in three provinces helped by providing information. The total number of prisoners in these institutions was more than 40,000, and all of these institutions responded to his request for information about their programs. Many gave extensive replies and were able to provide the photographs that we include. For a summary review of what prisons offer, please see the extensive table that begins on page 71.

It will be helpful to read his descriptions of various programs to see which programs or aspects of programs might be replicated in your setting. At the end of the work, he lists personal resources for individuals to contact. These people listed have been active in setting up their programs and may help you learn from their mistakes so you will be able to launch or expand your programs without as many problems as you might have had without their expert guidance. He also provides a broad bibliography for further research.

We realize the importance of correctional and community programs for children of incarcerated parents. We also recognize the importance of parenting programs in correctional settings—prisons, jails, boot camps, and other facilities. Based on our experience, we believe that if more individuals are taught how to be good parents, we can stem the rise of juvenile crime.

James A. Gondles, Jr.
Executive Director
American Correctional Association

Introduction

Since the publication of *Prisons and Kids* in 1985, both the number of new prisons constructed and the number of men and women incarcerated have increased dramatically. In the past decade, the number of women imprisoned in the United States has tripled, and this has resulted in a "building binge" (Chesney-Lind and Immarigeon 1995). In the 1970s, seventeen prisons were built; in the 1980s, thirty-four women's units or prisons were built, according to these writers.

The number of adults held in state or federal prisons or in local jails has increased over the past decade, and this increase has affected women inmates the most (Bureau of Justice Statistics 1986, 1987, 1995a, 1995c, 1995d). Comparing 1984 with 1994 (Bureau of Justice Statistics 1995d) reveals the following:

- 674,400 white male prisoners in 1994 represent a 91.7 percent increase over those incarcerated in 1984.
- 50,700 white female prisoners in 1994 represent a 166.8 percent increase—or 2.67 times the number incarcerated in 1984.
- 683,200 black male prisoners in 1994 represent a 140.2 percent increase—or 2.40 times the number incarcerated in 1984.
- 52,000 black female prisoners in 1994 represent a 207.7 percent increase—or 3.08 times the number incarcerated in 1984.

As funds for programs for prisoners are reduced, volunteer programs to support the families of the prisoners have attempted to fill this gap. A section on "Family Advocacy" briefly describes this movement.

In writing the original *Prisons and Kids* and this new and revised version, this researcher attempts to present a balanced picture of the issues related to incarcerated parents and their children. Although the emphasis in the literature is on mothers in prisons, much can be applied to incarcerated fathers, also. Programs for parents in jails is not covered in this publication, but this subject involves many of the same issues (Harris 1996). (Only the Prison MATCH program at the San Francisco County Jail number seven is described).

This book reports on the programs for incarcerated mothers in seventy-four state prisons, nine federal facilities, and three Canadian prisons in three provinces. The total number of women prisoners in these institutions is 40,758 (compared to 15,337 women in these prisons surveyed in 1984). The survey in this edition attempted to question authorities in all prisons housing women in the United States and Canada.

The present study surveys programs for incarcerated mothers and their children in all fifty states, the District of Columbia, and Canada. We obtained information by telephone interviews or questionnaires sent to correctional officials at state and federal institutions, and to Canadian prisons housing women, in December 1995 through April 1996. This study also includes findings from literature reviews of works in sociology, psychology, psychiatry, social work, law, child development, criminal justice, and corrections.

While the original study began as a survey of day care centers and nurseries in correctional institutions, it soon became clear that the topic of incarcerated parents and their children also includes visitation policies and procedures, family units, and conjugal visits, community facilities, supportive services for inmates with children, and even penal colonies. The range of programmatic options and state experiences with their use are described in Chapter 2, along with a table and section summarizing the results of the survey. Chapter 3 contains a discussion of some of the legal issues involved, and new sections on permanency planning and medical care. The latter deals with HIV and AIDS, problems that were not mentioned in 1985. Chapter 4 provides a context for decision making by exploring some of the issues regarding programs for inmates and their children. Chapter 5 contains a table that summarizes the information gathered from the survey. Chapter 6 includes policy statements on parenting programs from the American Correctional Association, the Federal Bureau of Prisons, and a copy of the Uniform Law Commissioners' Model Sentencing and Corrections Act. Chapter 7 provides an extensive bibliographical reference list and Chapter 8 provides contacts (names and addresses of persons who have contributed to this publication), and community programs and resources. It lists some of the many volunteer and family advocacy programs and individuals that assist former prisoners and their families in the community.

1. Parental Ties

Should infants and young children live in correctional institutions with their incarcerated mothers? Do bonding and parenting play a role in rehabilitation? What can correctional institutions realistically provide for inmates and their families?

Questions surrounding programs for incarcerated mothers and their children are controversial and emotional for both the public and correctional administrators. On the one hand, advocates stress the need to maintain a strong mother-child relationship through the child's early development. On the other, opponents cite administrative difficulties in offering programs for inmates' children. They argue that it is wrong to subject an innocent child to imprisonment because of a parent's crime.

"Establishing family services in prisons and jails is a controversial issue," Couturier (1995) states. Corrections' professionals, he contends, do not view families as legitimate clients and do not welcome the "intrusion of family members, volunteers, and outside agency personnel in their facilities." Citizens resent the "money and creature comforts afforded inmates . . . At the same time, many practitioners and researchers have identified a clear need for enhanced family services in jails and prisons to help inmates maintain contact with their families, reduce familial breakup and limit the social isolation that can accompany incarceration" (citing Hairston and Lockett 1987).

Despite lengthy experience with a variety of approaches since the 1950s, there is no consensus among correctional officials on how best to handle arrangements for incarcerated mothers and their children. Administrators do agree the inmate-child relationship should be maintained and strengthened, if possible. However, the availability and types of programs seem to depend on individual institutions and political realities.

Bonding

A recent report on child development (United States Department of Health and Human Services 1996) states, "The prospect that routine nonmaternal care in the first year of life might adversely affect the security of the infant's attachment to mother has been a subject of much discussion and debate over the past decade and a half, and discussion and debate continue to this day." While such controversy exists in this area when the research involves the general population, not surprisingly, even more uncertainty and controversy exists when the topic is incarcerated mothers and fathers and their children. The latter topic has been the subject of even less research.

The issue of bonding between mother and child is central to all arguments concerning prison nurseries, visitation, child custody, or inmate rights concerning children. Reflected in such concepts as the "tender years' doctrine," "maternal presumption," and "best interests of the child," the literature advocating programs for incarcerated mothers consider the mother-child bond to be the philosophical foundation for institutional and community programs.

The assumption is that bonding is critical for healthy development and emotional growth, and that its absence has many undesirable consequences for the child. Wooldredge and Masters (1993) cite some of the literature that describes some of the negative consequences resulting from the absence of a "continuous, intimate relationship" between a mother and her infant "during the first two years after birth."

Other assumptions involve the benefits of bonding for the incarcerated mother. Many persuasively argue that caring for an infant has a positive impact on rehabilitation by enhancing a mother's self-esteem, easing her guilt and anxiety about separation, and providing an opportunity for integrating her identity. Kimbrell (1994) states the argument succinctly:

> For a mother in prison, the strongest incentive for rehabilitation is to be reunited with her children when she is released. This bond is also critical for the child.

However, others argue that incarcerated mothers "exaggerate their maternal solicitude" and "often express very unrealistic and ideological perceptions of their maternal role" (Stanton 1980). Hungerford (1993), in his research on inmate mothers at the Franklin Pre-Release Center in Columbus, Ohio, writes that inmate mothers "have exaggerated self images as loving and concerned mothers and unrealistic expectations for positive reunification

with their children." Baunach made a similar observation. After studying the effects of separation of inmate mothers from their children, Baunach (1982, 1984) cited an advantage of separation:

> For some mothers, an additional impact of the separation is to heighten their understanding of their own behavior and its effects on their children. Especially for mothers who had been involved in drugs or alcohol for prolonged periods, incarceration provided them with a chance to step back and take stock of the experiences their children have endured (1979, p.121).

The bonding issue encompasses both neonatal contacts and mother-child separation. A 1976 book by Klaus and Kennell gave rise to the popular belief in the benefits of early physical contact between mothers and newborns—a view formally endorsed by the American College of Obstetrics and Gynecology and the American Hospital Association.

Chess and Thomas (1982) wrote:

> In middle-class American society, the mother-infant relationship is invested with a special mystique, both in the mass media and the professional literature. In the marketplace, the image of the blissful, nurturing mother with a happy, contented baby is used as a symbol of all that is desirable and good; by juxtaposition, these qualities are presumably transferred to the advertised product, whether it is soap or automobiles.
>
> In the mental health field, the concept of the decisive importance of the mother for the infant's development took hold gradually, starting in the 1920s with Freud's and Watson's emphasis on the paramount importance of the first years of life (p. 213).

By the 1970s, however, Chess and Thomas note frequent challenges to the professional ideology that held parents, "primarily the mother, all-responsible for their child's devel-

opmental course." By the mid-1970s, the new consensus was that although the mother is important, the child's development is subject to other influences such as "the father, siblings, the pattern of family organization and function, school, peer groups, larger social environment, and the child's own characteristics" (Chess and Thomas 1982, p. 215).

Lamb (1982) concluded, " . . . the studies . . . show no clear evidence for any lasting effect of early physical contact between mother and infant on subsequent maternal behavior. The most that can be said is that it may sometimes have modest short-term effects in some mothers in some circumstances." Brody (1983) noting a change in Klaus' position, quotes Klaus:

> . . . Rather, I'd say there is a suggestion that for some mothers additional contact in the first hours and days of life may be helpful and in some it may have a profound effect on how they care for the baby, especially poor mothers with few social supports. Right now, there are no studies that confirm or deny the presence of a sensitive period or that measure how much contact is needed between mother and baby during the first hours or days of life to have an effect.

In studies of British families and the long-term effects of different kinds of separation, such as working mothers, transient separation (illness or holidays), and permanent separations (death, divorce, or separation), Rutter (1971) concluded:

> Separation experiences have some association with the later development of antisocial behavior, but this is due not to the fact of the separation itself, but rather to the family dis-

> cord which precedes and accompanies the separation (p. 256).

Furthermore, Rutter (1979) found that a good relationship with one parent can help mitigate the effects of a poor family situation characterized by discord. He summarized some of the research on maternal deprivation and concluded:

> New research has confirmed that, although an important stress, separation is not the crucial factor in most varieties of deprivation. Investigations have also demonstrated the importance of a child's relationship with people other than his mother. Most important of all, there has been the repeated finding that many children are not damaged by deprivation.

Gaudin (1984), citing Ainsworth (1973), offers a similar conclusion:

> . . . Recent studies in child development have indicated that developmental effects of the extended physical separation of young children from their mothers are conditioned by several other variables. One of these is the quality of the substitute child care provided during the period of separation. The ill effects of separation can be greatly mitigated or eliminated, especially for infants, when a substitute parent figure offers consistent nurturing, stimulation, and individual attention to the young child.

In 1954, Margaret Mead summarized the state of knowledge in remarks foretelling Rutter's views twenty years later:

> At present, the specific biological situation of the continuing relationship of the child to its biological mother and its need for care by human beings are being hopelessly confused in the growing insistence that child and biological mother, or mother surrogate, must never be separated, that all separation, even for a few days, is inevitably damaging, and that if long enough it does irreversible damage. This, as Hilde Bruch (1952) has cogently pointed out, is a new and subtle form of antifeminism in which men—under the guise of exalting the importance of maternity—are tying women more tightly to their children than has been thought necessary since the invention of bottle feeding and baby carriages. Actually, anthropological evidence gives no support at present to the value of such an accentuation of the tie between mother and child. On the contrary, cross-cultural studies suggest that adjustment is most facilitated if the child is cared for by many warm, friendly people.

The following factors should be considered in assessing the effects of separations and other changes in the domestic life of children (Richards 1992):

- the meaning of the events for the child
- the quality of the children's relationships with those in their immediate social circle
- the factors that may alter consequences for their material well-being and wider social world
- many other factors such as the child's age, gender, and personality

Richards adds, in spite of a "growing series of descriptive studies of the consequences of imprisonment for families," "systematic follow-up studies of children" and "studies of the longer-term effects of parental imprisonment for children" are lacking. He concludes, "We cannot expect societal attitudes to change overnight, but we may be able to improve some situations for children by encouraging the wider family and friends to offer more practical help and support." Although he is writing about British society and attitudes, these comments also may be applied to the United States.

Regarding the controversies surrounding the subject of maternal deprivation (Rutter, 1995a):

- Most of the disorders usually associated with maternal deprivation appear to be associated with both genetic and environmental factors.
- Although early concepts of maternal deprivation included the notion that infancy constituted a critical period, with the ill effects of adverse parental care relatively immutable, this view has been dropped by almost all leading theorists . . . It is probable that different age periods will be important for different effects or different types of experiences.
- . . .(The initial) claims of the effects of maternal deprivation suggested that the effects were relatively immutable and not reversible by later experiences. "The early evidence was flawed by its failure to take account of environmental influences in later childhood and adolescence.
- There are individual and gender differences in responses to psychosocial stress and adversity.

Rutter concludes:

> What has stood the test of time most of all has been the proposition that the qualities of parent-child relationships constitute a central aspect of parenting, that the development of social relationships occupies a crucial role in personality growth, and that abnormalities in relationships are important in many types of psychopathology. It is evident that, as knowledge has advanced, so the questions to be tackled have extended in range and complexity. Such is the way of science.

Rutter's recent findings (1995b) decisively reject the traditional psychoanalytic theory of development as put forward by either Freud or Klein. If the evidence requires a rejection of the psychoanalytic postulates of drive, of psychosexual stages, and of fixation and regression, there would seem to be little point in persisting with the fiction that psychoanalysis offers any useful understanding of developmental processes. It is time that the theory was given a respectful burial, but dismissed with respect to its contemporaneous value. However, Rutter notes that recent texts continue to refer to these "outmoded" psychoanalytic concepts. His other ideas follow:

- Most authorities generally accept the idea that "children cope well with having several adults look after them provided that it is the same adults over time and provided that the individuals with whom they have a secure attachment relationship are available at times when they are tired, distressed or facing challenging circumstances.
- . . .(T)he original notion that children could not form initial selective attachments after the supposed sensitive period of the first two years has proved mistaken.
- One specific issue concerns decisions on how and when children need to be removed from their biological parents when they are being abused or neglected. All would accept that it is extraordinarily difficult to decide when the qualities of parental care are so bad that it is necessary to remove the child. Considerations of parent-child relationships are important but it is clear that considerations concerning safety, security, and the adequacy of care also are crucial. Appreciation

of the difficulties of providing all that is needed in good parenting in conditions of foster care and residential care need to be taken into account. Nevertheless, what is important is attention to the child's relationships with those who constitute his social family and not concern with some hypothetical 'blood bond.'

- . . . although there are very definite hierarchies in selective attachments, it is usual for most children to develop selective attachments with a small number of people who are closely involved in child care, and that social development is affected by later, as well as earlier relationships.
- The simplistic 'SuperGlue' notion of maternal bonding has fortunately passed into oblivion. Nevertheless, it is necessary that we do not lose sight of the various important factors that may foster and facilitate the development of parents' relationships with their babies.

The Father's Role

While emphasis in this publication and the literature is on the inmate mother, parenting opportunities for inmate fathers also should be considered (see R. Shaw 1987). There is a need for more research on incarcerated fathers and their children (Baunach 1979).

The special service needs of incarcerated fathers include: parental empowerment, services supporting father-child reunification and "services directed toward the root causes of domestic conflict and interpersonal violence, as well as services that assist prisoners and their families in achieving peaceful reunification" (Johnston and Gabel 1995).

Traditionally, child abuse prevention and treatment efforts do not focus on fathers who are in prison and their children. However, the Parents in Prison program at the Tennessee State Prison for Men does. It includes: home study courses, structured classroom courses, monthly special events including rap sessions with guest speakers and special projects, such as a Christmas banquet and a summer picnic (Hairston and Lockett 1985).

The goals of the program are "to strengthen, encourage, and improve parent-child relationships and to prevent child abuse and neglect." This program ". . . could be used in strengthening mothers' parental roles and skills as well." One of the key features of the program is the central coordinating committee which allows inmates to "develop and utilize leadership skills that can be transferred to community settings." The authors conclude, "The need for an impact evaluation of Parents in Prison cannot be overstated. Groups that elect to use this model for child abuse and neglect prevention need to know if it, indeed, makes a difference."

The paternal role in theories of child development historically has been neglected (Sack 1977). He cites a finding by Rutter (1971) that boys were more likely to show psychiatric disorders if it were the father rather than the mother who died or was ill. However, Rutter also wrote, "It may be that the importance of the same-sexed parent is marked only at certain ages, perhaps in adolescence." Sack called for more research, suggesting that parental discord may be more important with boys than with girls and that boys appear to be more vulnerable to psychological and biological stress than girls.

A program to meet the needs of families of incarcerated men at the Washington State Reformatory at Monroe was started in 1973. It provided family education, early childhood education, and children's activities (Taylor and Durr 1977). The program has changed considerably since then and currently consists of a marriage encounter program, parenting program, extended family visit program, and seminars that deal with family relationships, according to the Associate Superintendent of Program Services, Willie Daigle.

The Prisoners' Rights Sourcebook also recognizes the parental rights of male inmates:

> Although the emphasis here is on women prisoners, it is not in any way suggested that male prisoners should not be afforded the same rights in regard to their children as are women. Children should be allowed to visit their fathers as well. Fathers should not be deprived of their custody rights either (Herman and Haft 1973, pp. 346-7).

Based on a sample of 126 men in two southeastern prisons in a metropolitan area Hairston (1995) concludes:

> . . . programs and services that are developed based on traditional models of a two-parent, white, middle class family and using complex parent education reading materials will leave the majority of fathers in prison unaffected. [Because of their experiences and characteris-

tics they] can be expected to have limited interest in and use for complex reading materials that do not reflect understanding of their own culture, experiences, and lifestyles.

In a comparison of eight stressors between female and male inmates, Harris (1993) found that females experienced less stress than male inmates on seven of the eight dimensions. However, she points out that " . . . most female inmates have very limited access to their children making it difficult to maintain mother-child relationships. This is certainly a stressor not measured."

A study based on 302 inmates at the Eastern New York Correctional Facility examined "the manner and degree to which incarcerated fathers and their children interact" (Lanier 1991). The interaction was labeled "proximal" (Family Reunion Program participants, day visits, and attendance at Family Day picnics) or "distal" (exchange of cards and/or letters and telephone calls). The study points out that previous research has attributed the lack of proximal interaction to the great distances, the prohibitive costs, the absence of transportation, or the uncooperativeness of caregivers. This research suggests another factor: an absence of a depth of commitment to the relationship if the fathers did not live with their children prior to their imprisonment. The study also "underscored the importance of exchanging mail as a mode of interaction among incarcerated fathers and their children."

In a comparison of seventy incarcerated mothers with sixty-two incarcerated fathers in Kentucky prisons, Koban (1983) found the following:

- Female offenders have closer relationships with their children prior to incarceration than do men.
- Women's relationships with their children are more affected by incarceration.
- Women prisoners experienced a "significant disadvantage" compared to male prisoners in attempting to maintain consistent contact with their children and the caregivers of these children, and this resulted in problems during reunification with their children.
- While more mothers than fathers received at least one visit from their children during incarceration, the frequency of parent-child visits decreased after one year for the mothers, while it remained stable for the fathers.

Koban concludes:

Task forces, commissions, conferences, and publications are beginning to examine the special issues affecting imprisoned women . . . There also appears to be a growing recognition that experience with the criminal justice system is intergenerational and that the children of incarcerated parents may be at greater risk than their peers for future involvement with the criminal justice system . . . Coordinated efforts should be taken by the criminal justice and child welfare systems to ensure that mothers and their children are able to sustain their relationships.

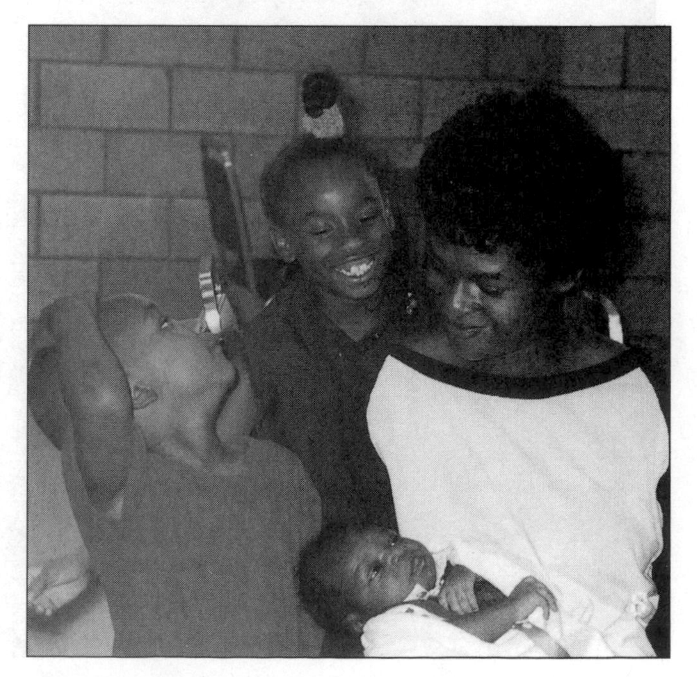

These comments by Hairston and Koban apply to both incarcerated mothers and fathers.

Woodrow (1992) in concluding her discussion of problems faced by the caregivers, the children, and the incarcerated mothers in Britain (which are similar to those in the United States) quotes R. Shaw (1987): "The children of imprisoned fathers can be identified at the bottom of the 'pecking order,' as one of the most deprived if not the most deprived group in our society." Nevertheless she adds, ". . . children of female inmates must lay claim to the latter status."

R. Shaw (1992b) also writes, however:

> It is important to make the point that occasionally a man's influence on his family can be so damaging and negative that his incarceration is quite likely to be beneficial to the children. Imprisonment can also provide a respite in an unsatisfactory marriage or give a woman the opportunity to escape with her children from a damaging or perhaps violent relationship which she was fearful of doing while he was at liberty. Marriages apparently broken by imprisonment should not, therefore, always be seen as an undesirable consequence of incarceration . . . However, such cases were in the minority in the study and imprisonment of a father must generally be viewed as an event likely to be painful and detrimental to any children involved.

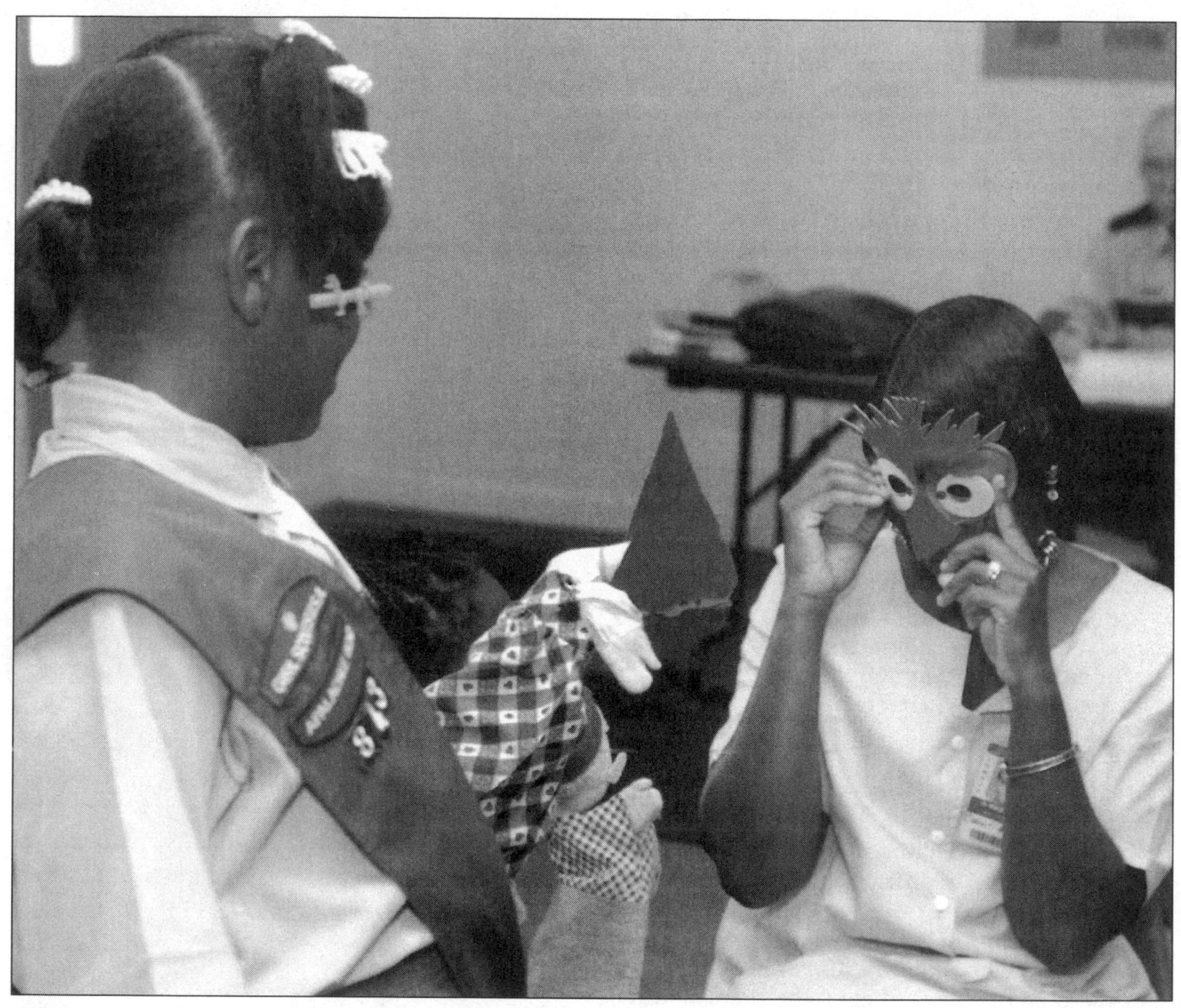

Photo used with permission from Girl Scouts Behind Bars.

2. Programs

Correctional experts and others recognize the need for programs for incarcerated parents and their children, but their reasoning has been as varied as the programs. At one end of a continuum of programs developed for the children of incarcerated mothers are prison nurseries. At the other end is care of the children by extended family members (including the grandparent, father, and other relatives) or placements in foster care. Usually, in the case of foster care, preferable placements are in the community near the facility where the mother is incarcerated. When this is possible, normal visitation rules should be eased so children may play and interact with their mothers in a day care center or children's center.

Between the intimacy of prison nurseries and the distance of foster care placement lies a variety of other arrangements for inmates and their children. This chapter discusses the range of alternative programs. "A variety of [visiting] schemes have been pioneered in Canada and the U.S. for keeping mothers and children in touch during the sentence and mothers responsibly involved with their children, which as yet have no equivalent in Britain" (Catan 1992).

Problems with Facilities

A 1991 survey of wardens of state prisons for women listed some of the problems that "have yet to be dealt with in any of the facilities" (Wooldredge and Masters 1993):

- adequate resources to deal with false labors, premature births, and miscarriages
- lack of maternity clothes
- pregnant inmates sometimes required to wear belly chains when being transported to the hospital
- minimum security pregnant inmates sometimes housed in maximum security facilities
- no place for a mother and her baby to remain together, or even separate visiting areas for mothers and newborn children
- often crowded living conditions

Recidivism Reduction

In a survey of policies on inmate-family communications in 1988, responses came from forty-one states, the District of Columbia, Guam, and the Virgin Islands. After reviewing these policies, the survey authors (Hairston and Hess 1989) concluded:

> These data indicate a wide variation in policy, broad discretion regarding visit practice, and severe restrictions to access. Overall, they reflect a systemwide problem with serious implications for family-oriented programs. Without greater vision and direction at the highest policy levels, the goals of strengthening family relationships during incarceration, reunifying families upon release, and reducing recidivism remain largely illusory.

Based on Hairston's review (1992) of research on prisoner-family ties and the institutional programs that serve to maintain these ties, her "future research agenda" includes the need to conduct research examining the "causal links" between the family environment and recidivism. Yet others conclude that there is a strong and consistently positive relationship between parole success and the maintenance of strong family ties (Holt and Miller 1972).

The development and expansion of family support programs have far outpaced the availability of research information on program implementation and effectiveness. This is a field where science has not played a major role in informing practice (Powell 1994).

Glasser (1990, 1993) describes her evaluation of the parenting programs at the Connecticut Correctional Institution at Niantic. The program (in 1987 to 1990) consisted of "support and educational groups, a child centered visiting center" (the "Sesame Street" program), "training for inmates to work with children in the visiting center, weekend trailer visits for women and their children, creative arts for mothers and children, and referrals for community services." Although the qualitative data based on interviews with the women were very positive, the quantitative data led to the following conclusion:

> It was not possible to demonstrate that these positive benefits of the parenting programs were able to reduce the woman's chances of coming back to prison when compared with the total population . . . (Glasser 1993).

Wide variations exist in the programs available to incarcerated parents and their children, as shown in the following information.

Prison Nurseries

A survey of administrators at forty-four state institutions for women and four federal institutions found opinion divided on the subjects of prison nurseries and whether children should live in the institutions (Association on Programs for Female Offenders 1981). Asked to indicate their support for the following statements: a) "Children should never be allowed to stay overnight in prison with their psychological mother," 25 percent strongly agreed. "Children should be allowed to visit with their psychological mothers overnight whenever desirable," 4 percent partially agreed; 31 percent strongly agreed; 15 percent partially agreed; and 25 percent were undecided.

On another pair of opposing statements, "Prisons should not have nurseries," 25 percent strongly agreed; while 31 percent strong-

ly agreed that "Prisons should have nurseries," and 17 percent partially agreed that they should, while 21 percent were undecided.

Prison nurseries where infants may stay following birth exist in North Carolina, Ohio, Pennsylvania, and perhaps other states, but at these institutions the infants usually are housed in the prison infirmary until arrangements can be made for placement of the child with foster parents or other caregivers. Although placement of the infant may take several weeks or even months, housing at the institution is considered only a temporary situation.

In 1981, the Federal Correctional Institution at Alderson, West Virginia, was the only all-female federal institution in the United States. A contract with the state of West Virginia provided for the incarceration of female offenders under the state's jurisdiction. A nursing home for the elderly was used to house incarcerated pregnant women two months before the birth of their babies and two months after the birth for purposes of "bonding," provided the women had a relatively short time remaining on their sentences. The program was discontinued when the nursing home no longer had space available for the incarcerated mothers.

Foreign Programs

Glasser (1993) summarizes some of the literature on prisons for mothers or fathers and their children in Canada, the United Kingdom, India, Nepal, Chile, Costa Rica, Thailand, and other countries. The conditions he describes in some of these countries, specifically in Thailand and Nepal, are appalling. The author concludes: "Research that attempts to measure the results of various programs and policies should be widely publicized to prisons and the public throughout the world."

The Preungesheim Prison in Frankfurt, West Germany, built a Children's Home in 1975 at a cost of $800,000. Its capacity was twenty women and up to twenty-five of their children, ranging from infants to children up to six years of age (Newsweek 1976, Greening 1978). The program had two objectives: to keep detrimental influences from the children and keep the children with their mothers, and to aid in healing children both physically and mentally. The Children's Home was staffed by five correctional officers, four nurses, a cook who also taught cooking to the inmate mothers, and two social workers. The house was physically separate from the rest of this maximum- security institution. From 1975 to 1978, 91 women and 108 children were housed at the Children's Home. Of that group, only one recidivist has been reported.

Douglas (1993) provides a thorough description of this program and its history at Frankfurt. The present Children's Home, or "Mutter-Kind-Heim," was opened in 1988. There are two Mutter-Kind-Heim prisons at this four-prison complex; one is "closed" and the other is "open." There are also a "closed" men's prison and a "closed" women's prison. The closed women's prison has five mothers and their children; the mothers work in the complex during the day while their children are at the open unit of the Children's Home. At the open Children's Home, there are eighteen inmate mothers and their children. These mothers work outside of the prison and return at 5:00 p.m. to prepare dinner for their children. During the day, the children are cared for and taken on trips by trained "educators."

The inmate mothers may leave the Children's Home with their children until 8:00 P.M.; if they can arrange for someone to care for their children, the mothers may leave again and return in time for the 10:00 P.M. lockdown. A mother may have two or more

children with her until they are six years of age, but a recent Swedish study recommends that the children leave by the age of three. In four years, the institution reports that no mothers have been returned, and the director states that the overall recidivism rate of the mothers since 1975, is "almost nil."

When released, a mother is eligible for state aid of about $285 per month for the mother, $153 per month for each child, and rent-free housing. (These estimates are based on the amounts given by Douglas in 1993 and the exchange rate in March 1996). However, there is a housing shortage in Germany. Other problems described by Douglas are AIDS (in the main women's prison at Frankfurt 30 percent of the women are HIV positive); and because of the mother's "absolute right to deliver her child to whomever she chooses outside the prison," there may be instances when the child is cared for by an inappropriate person.

In France, "Each year fifty to sixty children under the age of eighteen months are accepted into the prisons for an average stay of six months (Trabut 1993). There are no provisions for children older than eighteen months, but this is being studied. At Fleury-Megoris, the "best organized" of the twelve institutions, there is a day-nursery that is separated from the prison, and it accommodates seventeen mothers and their children. The decision to have the child in prison is made by the custodians of the child and not by prison authorities. The mother is in charge of all decisions pertaining to the health and socialization of the family and her child. The "goal is to empower women to assume their responsibility as mothers, and secondly, to create more links to the community."

Trabut explains there are alternatives to incarceration due to "the fact that children do not belong in prison. There are other ways of avoiding incarceration that would allow for the social control of the offender, such as parole. . . . The fundamental right of each person, including the incarcerated mother, to have a family life is one of the essential conditions integral to successful reintegration," Trabut concludes.

Catan (1992) conducted research at three "prison mother and baby units" at three British institutions for women, HMP Styal, Holloway, and Askham Grange. These units provide places for thirty-nine babies—up to the age of nine months at Styal and Holloway and up to eighteen months at Askham. The average stay for the infants was thirteen weeks in Holloway, seventeen weeks in Styal, and nineteen weeks at Askham Grange. In her review of the literature, Catan writes that "issues about prisoners' babies" have been "formulated by applying child development theories in a rather general, and inaccurate, way."

The research consisted of comparing the development of seventy-four babies who lived in the prison mother and baby units in April 1986 to October 1988 with thirty-three babies of similar ages who were cared for in the community during their mothers' imprisonment. The infants were tested on a monthly basis and during a three-month period after the mothers' release. Some of the main findings and ideas contained in Catan's paper are the following:

- (I)t is not being in a prison mother and baby unit per se that raises issues, nor being separated from an imprisoned mother, but that issues arise concerning the preventable experiences that frequently attend or follow on from these alternatives.
- While no severe and general developmental effects were found among the children in the prison units, "babies who spent longer than average in the units revealed a gradual developmental decline over a four-month period, compared with those separated from the mother for a similar length of time." The declines were in only two areas, locomotor and cognitive.

Mother and baby units in prisons should:

- offer opportunities for babies to practice and elaborate their basic skills of locomotor and cognitive development
- allow free movement and elaborative exercise by the infants
- provide educational toys, playdough, finger painting, etc., and other activities that offer novelty and stimulation
- employ properly trained staff. "Even the best-intentioned of adults" tend to "revert to neat, ordered, and relatively bare environments and to restrict inmates' movement around the various locations within the institution . . . Most of the adults' activities with the babies were classified as care, comfort, social interaction, and loving, while educational, guided, and exploratory play were comparatively infrequent."

"There were no developmental decrements in the separated babies and this indicated that the quality of care given by relatives and foster parents compensated for the experience of separation from their mothers." However, some of the difficulties uncovered by the research were the following:

- stress due to various factors experienced by the caregivers
- "the ad hoc, unstable nature of the child care arrangements"
- infrequent contacts between the children and their mothers in prison

Catan concludes:

> Thus, if we wish to know whether the infants of imprisoned mothers are likely to be similarly at risk of future delinquency or offending, we should not ask about the effects of maternal imprisonment per se, but rather examine whether the families of women prisoners possess the characteristics that comprise the 'culture of poverty,' increasing the difficulty of good parenting.

If the children of imprisoned women are at risk of deviant behavior in the long term, these children and their families who possess "multiple disadvantages require a broad array of coordinated social and economic policies," according to Catan.

Other countries offer nurseries for children of incarcerated inmates. In Japan, reportedly, incarcerated mothers may keep their children in the institution up to the age of one year (conversation with the author, M. Hess 1983). In Bolivia, nursing infants, and in Venezuela children up to three years of age are permitted to stay with their incarcerated mothers.

> In Colombia, incarcerated pregnant women are required by law to leave prison in the seventh month of pregnancy and to return to complete their sentences when the infant is two months old. In reality, however, few women return and the law is not enforced. It is for this reason that women reportedly are disallowed sexual activity on prison grounds. Such behavior leads to pregnancy, which is ultimately a "ticket" to free society (Goetting 1984, p. 12).

North American Experiences

The "Babies Behind Bars" program was initiated about 1980 at the Portage Correctional Institution for Women in Portage la Prairie, Manitoba, Canada. It allows newly born babies to remain with their mothers in prison for up to one year of age.

In the United States, some states—Florida, Illinois, Kansas, Massachusetts, Pennsylvania, and Virginia—have had nurseries and/or laws mandating nurseries for the children of incarcerated mothers, but their programs no longer are in operation. Circumstances regarding their discontinuation are summarized below on a state-by-state basis. In addition, some states have nurseries or community facilities where mothers can live with their children—as in California, Minnesota, Nebraska, South Dakota, and New York—and these also are described.

California. Section 3401 of the California Code, passed in 1919, allowed an incarcerated mother to keep her child(ren) with her in the institution up to the age of two years. The statute allowed the Department of Corrections discretionary authority to make this decision, and policy review allowed a mother to keep her child with her while incarcerated at the California Institution for Women at Frontera. This policy was challenged in 1976 in *Cardell v. Enomoto* in California Superior Court, but discretionary authority remained with the department, with denials allowed only on "reasonable grounds" (Star 1981).

The California Legislature passed Sections 3410-3424 of the California Penal Code, effective January 1, 1980. On the premise that "the prison was a poor place to keep infants," the statute established a community treatment program for incarcerated mothers and their children. The Community Prisoner Mother Program initially provided that a child remain with its mother up to the age of two years, but during the first year of implementation only six inmate mothers had been placed in community facilities with their children. The evaluation of this program concluded that eligibility requirements were too restrictive, accounting for low participation (Star 1981).

The legislation had a sunset clause calling for its expiration in mid-1982, but a new statute was passed in July 1982 (Assembly Bill 415 amended Sections 3411-3424), changing the maximum age of the child to six years and including more specific criteria. The program is still in operation (Sharrell Blakeley, letter of January 4, 1996). These mothers are "typically parolees or in the last months of their prison term."

Responding to the "dramatic increase in the number of incarcerated women who are single mothers or primary caretakers of children" and who have a history of substance abuse problems, the California Governor signed The "Pregnant and Parenting Women's Alternative Sentencing Program Act" on May 9, 1994. It authorizes the development of residential programs for mothers with a history of substance abuse and their children in San Diego, Los Angeles, Sacramento, and the San Francisco Bay Area (Alameda or San Francisco Counties).

The "Family Foundations Program—Mothers and Children Together" is an alternative to prison for those women who are considered eligible by the probation department, the district attorney, the sentencing judge, and the department of corrections. Each facility will treat twenty-five to thirty women and not more than two of her children for twelve months, and then for another twelve months that the mother is on intensive supervision parole. During this time, the following services will be available: substance abuse treatment, health care, individual and group therapy, parenting skills, education/life skills/

vocational training, infant and child development, and transition services to community living. Both the Community Prisoner Mother Program and the Family Foundations Program "strive for family reunification and the development of improved parenting, personal, and social skills" (Blakeley 1995).

Florida. From 1957 to 1975, babies were kept at the Florida Correctional Institution at Lowell (medium security) and at the Broward Correctional Institution (maximum security). Babies could remain there up to the age of eighteen months. Around 1975, the policy changed. Infants of women prisoners who gave birth were placed in foster homes directly from the community hospital and not brought to the prison. The statute was amended in 1979 and discretionary authority was given to the court to decide the "best interests of the child."

On March 22, 1979, inmate Terry Jean Moore gave birth to a child fathered by a correctional officer and petitioned the courts to force the institution to comply with the existing statute. That year the legislature passed a bill containing procedures for incarcerated mothers to request the court to decide whether they could keep their babies at the institution. Under that legislation, as many as ten children could be at the Florida Correctional Institution at Lowell at any one time. In 1981, the legislation was repealed; no babies were allowed to remain at the institution.

The following issues raised in *Wainwright v. Moore* (374 So. 2d 586, Florida District Court of Appeals, 1979) support incarcerated mothers keeping their children with them (Brodie 1982):

- In recognition of the importance of the mother-child bond, the mother should not be deprived of her right to maintain physical custody of her child.
- The bonding process is important to the mother's identity and self-image as a woman.
- The mother-child bond is critical to the infant's mental health and development.
- The future relationship between the mother and the child depends on the development of a bond during the child's first eighteen months. A breach in the bond may be irreparable.
- Predictions of negative consequences to a child who remains at a correctional institution to the age of twelve to eighteen months have not occurred in New York State, which "has had an ongoing program for the last forty years" (p. 682).

An aide of a Florida legislator who sponsored the repeal of this legislation summarized the reasons for the 1981 repeal:

1. A prison is not a normal environment and is not a place for children. The "normalcy" requirement referred to the absence of contacts with males at the women's institution, and the lack of opportunities for everyday activities such as visits to grocery stores, and other activities.
2. The security and liability were too much to assume, and the children could not be housed in a separate unit. There were concerns for the security of the infants.
3. The Florida Attorney General held that if a baby were killed by an inmate, the state would be held liable and could be sued.
4. The women were looking for special privileges in caring for the children, and there were no programs nor time for rehabilitation activities. References were made to mothers who prior to imprisonment had not cared for their children, or who were suspected of abuse resulting in a child's death.

5. The Department of Corrections could not function as a nursery or babysitting service.
6. The privilege resulted in animosities between inmates. For example, mothers whose babies were born prior to incarceration could not keep the children in prison, while others who gave birth after incarceration could keep their babies.
7. There was concern that the program catered to the best interests of the inmate mother rather than the best interests of the baby.
8. The Attorney General held that a separate facility was needed for security reasons. At first, the hospital was closed and used as housing for the mother and her infant. Later, cottages outside the prison were used until the statute was repealed.
9. No research evaluations or valid statistics were available on the results and effectiveness of such programs.

Reflecting on the Florida program, William E. Booth, former superintendent at the Lowell Institution, stated:

> The general opinion of the other inmates at the institution has fluctuated considerably, and probably as you expect, some inmates feel that babies should be allowed to stay here, others do not, and some care very little one way or the other, or at least they have not verbalized their individual opinion. It is my opinion, however, that in general the overall population at this institution has accepted the nursery program well and it has not caused a great deal of difficulty with the inmate mothers and their children.

Illinois. From 1927 to 1973, inmate mothers could keep their babies at the Dwight Correctional Center until age one unless there were "special reasons" for them to remain. This was replaced by a new statute in 1973 (Ch. 38-1003-6-3) that allowed the Department of Correction discretionary authority to handle the birth of infants at a facility as "necessary or appropriate." Subsequently, infants were not returned to Dwight on birth. Instead, prior to delivery, inmate mothers made arrangements for the care of their babies and, in the majority of cases, placed the children with immediate family members.

"A few" of the "numerous" problems cited in disallowing mothers to keep their babies at the institution included: inadequate housing, problems of health care, disciplinary actions and the segregation of inmate mothers, prerelease placement of the mother, and crowding of the institution.

Kansas. Kansas passed a statute (76-2506) in 1917 permitting the State Industrial Farm for Women at Lansing to house a child up to two years of age. According to some of the older inmates, when the population of the women's institution was smaller (about forty inmates), "there were more children than inmates."

The legislature repealed the statute, effective July 1, 1974, citing the following reasons:

1. The statute was not used between 1962 and 1973, and as part of the modernization of the code, it was repealed.
2. The state did not want to assume the risk to the child because the facilities were considered inadequate.
3. The expert opinion at the time was that it was bad for the child to be with the parent for two years and then face the trauma of separation.
4. The institution's population had increased and it had become crowded.

Massachusetts. Babies were allowed to stay with their mothers at the Massachusetts Correctional Institution at Framingham from 1858 to 1958. A female prisoner could have custody until the child reached the age of eighteen months. With some exceptions, children were allowed to remain until they were three years of age. During the time, that mothers were allowed to keep their children, a volunteer nursing organization came throughout the day. Mothers were expected to work with all other inmates daily, and take care of their children from approximately 6:00 P.M. until the following morning. Reasons cited for the repeal of this legislation included concerns about liability and "management problems."

Minnesota. "CAMP is a program for inmates who give birth while at the Minnesota Correctional Facility at Shakopee, who have four months or less before their Supervised Release Date at the time of the birth, and who will be parenting upon their return to the community." The mother and her infant are taken from the hospital to the ReEntry residential facility. While at ReEntry, the mother attends the Genesis II program for counseling and parenting classes. MCF Shakopee provides $40 per month for the mother's personal needs, and ReEntry provides $100 per month for the baby's needs. The mother's medical expenses are paid by MCF Shakopee, but the mother is responsible for the baby's medical expenses.

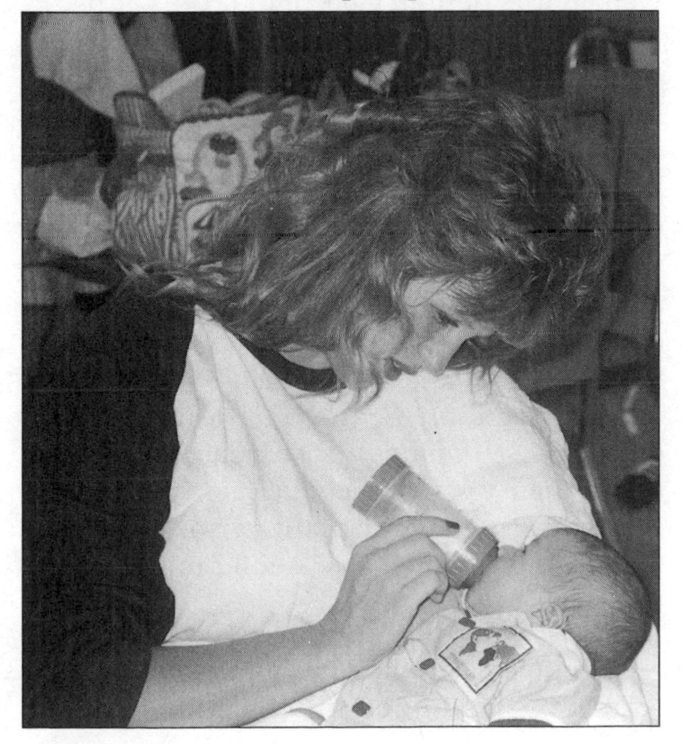

Nebraska. At the Nebraska Center for Women in York, Nebraska, the Nursery Unit allows a pregnant woman who is within eighteen months of her release, and who meets other requirements, to live in the unit with her infant until her release. While in the unit, the inmate mother must attend classes in the nursery and in the MOLD (Mother/Offspring Life Development) program.

New York. New York established a long-term nursery in 1901. The Taconic nursery was established across from the Bedford Hills Facility in 1990. The Bedford Hills facility has room for twenty-five inmate mothers and their children and the Taconic facility has twenty-three beds. Mothers are able to live with their infants until their children are one year old, and in some cases until eighteen months.

Sister Elaine Roulet, the director of The Children's Center, (Roulet et al., 1993), rebuts reasons given by state legislators to keep a nursery out of women's prisons.

> There is no question that the separations are traumatic for mother and child. We have written a number of pediatricians about this and read extensively hoping to learn the best moment for separation. There isn't one. It will vary from child to child.

Instead, she emphasizes the need for a broader use of alternatives to prison. However,

> To date, there has been no study made to determine how the program may have affected the child's future development. Since so many factors would enter into this, it would be a difficult study to make.

Pennsylvania. In response to an inquiry, the health care administrator of the State Correctional Institution at Murray described an event that occurred about thirty years ago:

> We have had only one experience with this situation. In this one case, when the baby was twenty-seven days old, she was transferred to her mother's cottage. It was stated that the mother was unable to make a home plan for this baby to her satisfaction and after several appeals to the superintendent was given special permission for this housing arrangement. The cottage she lived in had ample room and the inmate had two rooms: one for the baby and one for herself with a connecting bathroom.
>
> After the baby was one-month old and infant food was ordered by the physician, it was necessary for someone from the nursing staff to do the shopping for jarred baby food, juice, cereal, and fruit. This was necessary as these foods could not be procured in-house by requisition. It was a constant inconvenience to the nursing staff. Special arrangements also had to be made with the laundry to have the baby's clothes laundered, first thing in the morning before one washer was used for institutional laundry. The mother did not always have the dirty clothes ready, and this proved to be a handicap at the laundry. The mother very soon became bored with caring for the baby and manipulated other inmates to care for her. When the mother was assigned housework to do, she used the baby's care as a reason to be excused from a detail. She used the baby's presence to evoke sympathy and favors from staff as well as inmates. At the end of eight months there was much unrest in the cottage, and the baby was taken by the mother to a community living arrangement when she went on furlough (letter to the author from Harvey Bell, March 28, 1983).

South Dakota. The Springfield State Prison at Springfield, South Dakota has a Mother-Infant Program that is a division of the P.A.C.T. program (described elsewhere in this publication). The Mother-Infant program permits a female inmate who gives birth while incarcerated to keep the infant for a period of thirty days "to enable and to perpetuate the bonding of a mother-child relationship."

Virginia. In 1918, a Virginia statute allowed incarcerated mothers to keep their children up to the age of four. This was amended in 1930 to allow what is essentially the current statute authorizing the director of the Department of Corrections to decide whether a child should remain with its mother at the institution according to the best interests of the child (Brodie 1982).

Brodie was not able to obtain information on this program prior to 1943. From 1943 to the 1970s, women were permitted to keep their children until age two. Mothers could visit with their babies only on Sunday afternoons. As many as twenty-one babies were at the institution for women that was part of the men's penitentiary at Richmond until 1932, when the Virginia Correctional Center for Women was built in Goochland.

Most babies left the institution between the ages of nine and eighteen months. Their length of stay decreased to three months around 1964, and to thirty days in 1968. In 1976, a new superintendent arrived and discontinued the policy, contending: It was not in the best interests of either the infant or the mother. It would be easier for both mother and child "if the separation was made before they become attached to each other." The facilities were inadequate. It caused bitterness among other women inmates whose incarceration had forced them to leave their children behind.

Finally, he contended, the prison was not a "proper environment for a child in its formative years."

"The policy of not allowing the babies to return to the institution with their mothers has never been reduced to writing" (Brodie). No case has ever been litigated in Virginia challenging the director's authority to decide what is in the best interests of the child. According to Brodie:

> Virginia is at a crossroads. Its statute is not an accurate reflection of actual practice; in fact, the statutes and reality are diametrically opposed. There are clearly two options if the state wishes to correct the current situation: 1) the General Assembly can either repeal or revise the current statute; or 2) the Department of Corrections can formulate a policy that is in compliance with the statute . . . The policy should provide for an individualized hearing by the Director [who] would be able to make a case-by-case determination based on the facts of each case.

Buckles and LaFazia (1973) have commented that an inmate mother who is

> worried over or defending her role and rights as a mother has little time or energy left to participate in the counseling or rehabilitative resources available to her. Alleged or real injustices or hurts regarding their children are extremely effective red herrings that women can use to avoid personal issues.

However, focusing on the children involved, Hoffman (1977) expressed another view. "It is time we began to take steps to correct our mistakes: to fund experimental prison nurseries and carefully evaluate the emotional health of the children reared in them." Few correctional administrators appear willing to follow that suggestion, although everyone agrees on the need for more research and evaluation.

Children's Centers and Day Care Centers

In a paper on "prison visitors' centres" in Britain, Lloyd (1992) describes two movements in the past twenty-five years: prison visitors' centers and support organizations and self-help groups. In Britain, the first visitors' center was established in Birmingham in 1969. Based on her experience with "Save the Children," Lloyd believes the following are the core services that are essential at each center:

- play matched with the child's needs when a parent wishes to visit with his or her partner alone
- advice on child development and management of behavioral problems
- inexpensive food and drinks
- listening, counseling, and providing support for those who need someone to talk to
- "specialist advice and information" on the welfare, social service, and criminal justice systems
- general information on health, education, prisons, transport, visiting procedures, prisoners' allowances (parcels), etc.
- a system for linking families with sources of continuing support in their own communities

Many institutions have an area set aside for the children to play, adjacent to the visiting area, while the inmatc mother and visiting adults visit. The mother may use the area to play and interact with her child. The children's center may be equipped with donated toys or be supported by the Sesame Street television program through toys and borrowed characters.

MATCH and PATCH Programs

The National Council on Crime and Delinquency administered the Prison MATCH (Mothers And Their Children) program, established in 1978 at the Federal Correctional Institution at Pleasanton, California (Rosenkrantz and Joshua 1982). Instead of having an infant at the institution, it called for strengthening the mother-child bond through: improved conditions for visiting, inmate training in parenting and early childhood educa-

tion, improved prenatal care, and referrals for other social services.

Weilerstein (1995) provides a detailed description of the program, its history, and the changes the program has undergone (including the change to "Mothers, Fathers and Their Children"). However, in 1988 its contract at FCI-Pleasanton was not renewed.

In 1989, the Prison MATCH program was established at the San Francisco County Jail number seven, where it has components similar to those at Pleasanton, but with less involvement of the incarcerated parents in the administration of the program. These components include:

- The Children's Center where prisoners and their children from infancy to fifteen years of age can develop "parent-child bonds through play and learning activities"
- Supportive social services are provided and referrals are made to assist the parents with foster care and child custody issues, and crisis intervention
- Parents learn parenting skills by interaction and observation with volunteer staff, and other parents and their children. "Formal parenting classes are available throughout the jail."
- A nearby community college offers a human services training program. The program teaches paraprofessional skills to enable inmates to work with children and their families. This follows a self-help and peer-help model of supportive services.
- "Breaking the Intergenerational Cycle of Addiction" is a program funded by the Robert Wood Johnson Foundation and offers: supportive services, including individual and family counseling, postrelease planning, referrals, and follow-up.

Eleven states have replicated the Prison MATCH program in prisons and jails and three federal prisons in Alderson, West Virginia; Fort Worth, Texas; and Lexington, Kentucky (Weilerstein 1995).

The Prison PATCH program (Parents And Their CHildren) was established in 1984 and has visiting centers at both of the women's prisons in Missouri. The program provides transportation so that incarcerated mothers can visit with their children in a "homelike atmosphere." PATCH offers parenting classes that are sponsored through the Children's Trust Fund; individual counseling; liaison services with the division of family services and the juvenile courts; holiday and birthday programming for the children; and a speaker's bureau. Another component of the PATCH program is the Storytime Project. The incarcerated mother selects a child's book to read into a tape recorder. The book and tape are then sent to the children so that they have their mother's voice to listen to whenever they wish.

Some prisons have more elaborate programs with many facets. Some of the following programs involve several elements that may be of interest to those seeking a more well-rounded approach.

At Bedford Hills Correctional Facility in New York, the Children's Center has seven major departments (Roulet et al. 1993): The Children's Center, The Parenting Center, The Nursery, Infant Day Care, Prenatal Center, Child Advocacy Office, and the Taping Room. The program is funded by the State of New York and administered by the Catholic Charities, Diocese of Brooklyn. These departments offer a child development associate course for inmates; information and advice on foster care and other legal matters; contacts with families, schools, and agencies; parenting classes; bilingual parenting materials; and four buses each month from four of the boroughs of New York City, as well as an upstate bus that originates in Buffalo, New York.

The Dwight Correctional Center in Illinois has a Children's Visitation Center in the chapel area, which accommodates the visitation between mothers and their children up to age ten. This area is separate from but adjacent to the visiting room. The center allows for positive interaction between the mothers and their children. Although all mothers are encouraged to remain in the building if needed, they may return to the visiting room to visit with their adult visitors. The only other adults who are permitted to visit in the center are Department of Children and Family Services representatives or contract agency workers who are required to monitor their visits.

The Pennsylvania Department of Corrections has had a family services program since 1973, "when it established a children's center in the visiting room of the Pittsburgh penitentiary. Since that time, the state's family services have expanded to include children's centers, spousal groups, parenting and child development classes and other family-oriented activities." Its most comprehensive family services are at its two women's prisons. The department has plans for "a nursery, where women may deliver and interact with their babies outside of the prison setting, and community-based group residences, where mothers may raise their children. These community diversion programs are designed for women with shorter sentences who either are pregnant or have young children . . . Family services in the men's facilities are less elaborate." (Couturier 1995).

At the State Correctional Institution at Muncy, Pennsylvania, Project IMPACT (Inside Muncy Parents and Children Together), a nonprofit organization on contract to the Pennsylvania Department of Corrections, offers classes "for prenatal and developmental stages of children in both group settings and as independent studies." The program was developed in 1986 and is a "licensed mental health unit that provides psychological assessment, medical treatment, individual and group therapy, follow-up and outpatient care" (Clement 1993). This program is modeled after the Prison MATCH program.

The "purpose of the program is to strengthen the mother/child relationship through positive interaction. The children's center offers a place to visit in a comfortable, homelike environment. The center is open six days each week during the regular institution visiting hours" (according to information from the institution). The Project IMPACT has developed an interesting set of manuals to help parents stay in touch with their children's caregivers and educators, as well as provide a way for incarcerated parents to help their children in school.

At the State Correctional Institution at Cambridge Springs, Pennsylvania, a children's center is being developed and expects to be open by the fall of 1996. This modular unit also will house the parenting classes, offices, a fully-equipped kitchen, and an adjoining picnic area to be used when the weather permits.

Plans are underway to open a Family Preservation Center at the Indiana Women's Prison in Indianapolis, when funds have been approved for staffing. The center's focus will be on "developing and maintaining a strong bond" between offender mothers and their children. The project will include a child-friendly visiting area, and inform caregivers about the center. It also will assist mothers in developing parenting skills and will provide group counseling.

In Rhode Island, at the Adult Correctional Institutions/Women's Division at Cranston, the parenting program includes parenting education, and "a safe nurturing environment in which women and children can interact." According to the parenting coordinator, Alberta Baccari:

> Many of our children will not be reunified with their birth families and for this population the children's center provides the framework for building and storing positive memories of quality time with mom. For those children who will be reunited with family, our program provides the opportunity to maintain and strengthen the bond between mother and child.

Parenting Classes

About 97 percent, of the eighty-six institutions responding to the survey for this publication, offer classes on parenting and related subjects or were planning such courses. However, this figure may be exaggerated and include subjects not specifically designed for incarcerated mothers. In most states, inmates have an opportunity to enroll in such classes as child development, parenting skills, prenatal care, first aid, nutrition, child rearing, job opportunities, child abuse and neglect, family relations, and communications.

The North Carolina Correctional Institution for Women in Raleigh has a Prison MATCH program, a S.T.E.P. program (Systematic Training for Effective Parenting) for mothers of children of three different age groups, and a support group for pregnant inmates that provides education in prenatal and postnatal care through Wake County Health Department instructors. In addition, the Motheread Program was introduced at this institution to foster "healthy parenting and emotional well-being through innovative education classes that focus on story sharing with children." Students make book audio tapes that they send home to their children, learn parenting skills by discussing the stories' themes, and "develop their own writing skills by composing their own stories and letters to send home to their children" (Martin and Cotten 1995).

An evaluation of the Motheread Program by the School of Public Health at the University of North Carolina at Chapel Hill found that the program was "helpful to the inmates, regardless of whether one examines the women's literacy skills, parenting attitudes, or emotional health . . . Furthermore, there was statistically significant improvement in the women's parenting attitudes over the course of Motheread, with the women becoming more empathic with and responsive to their children's needs" (Martin and Cotten 1995).

A program similar to the Motheread Program is "Baby Ready/Baby Steps" at the Minnesota Correctional Facility at Shakopee. Some examples of other parenting classes are "Families and Self Esteem," "Parenting Teens," and "Parenting with Pride" ("a culturally sensitive approach to parenting").

Although not a parenting course, Girl Scouts Beyond Bars is a program that began in 1992 at the Maryland Correctional Institution for Women (Moses 1995, 1993). It is now in correctional institutions for women in Arizona, California, Delaware, Florida, Kentucky, Massachusetts, New Jersey, and Ohio. The program enables inmate mothers and their daughters to spend supervised time on arts and crafts projects and provides them with opportunities to learn about such topics as drug abuse, relationships, coping with family crises, teenage pregnancy prevention, and careers in math and science.

The Mother/Offspring Life Development (MOLD) program at the Nebraska Center for Women at York was "the first of its kind in the United States when it began in 1976. The program consists of overnight visits for inmate mothers and their children. Children may visit up to five nights per month. Classes are offered on the Lamaze method of childbirth, parenting, child development, health, self-esteem, and money management.

At the Columbia River Correctional Institution in Portland, Oregon, the co-educational facility has a family literacy program. The purpose of the program is to allow the children "to be with their parents in a positive educational setting." The children "come in on alternate Saturday mornings to read a storybook and participate in art activities around the theme of the book." The program is contracted with Portland Community College. Education manager, Julie Garvin, states, "I have very strong feelings about the importance of keeping already fragmented families together. I also believe that having a positive experience around education is important. Many of our residents have not liked school in their lives and pass that feeling onto their children."

The S.T.E.P. program also is offered at the Ohio Reformatory for Women at Marysville. "Upon completion of the program, participants are permitted two visits monthly in the parenting area, which is a homelike setting, including a picket fenced-in yard." Toys are available and snacks are served during these one-on-one visits. A separate waiting area is available for the caretakers during the visits, and television and reading materials are available for their use. The facility reports they have had 333 visits with caregivers, Children's Service caseworkers, inmate mothers and children during the calendar year. The parenting program also had Mom and Kid's Days in August and December 1995. "Each event lasted two four-hour days," and included planned activities, games, and lunch for about 425 participants each day at each event.

The Franklin Pre-Release Center in Columbus, Ohio has a Prenatal Program that includes "Lamaze Childbirth classes, fetal development, mothers' health issues, early childhood development, and exercise and pregnancy problems." The institution has a contract with Ohio State University Hospital Obstetrics/ Gynecology Clinic and "various county children's services agencies that facilitate the placement of the baby." A course on parenting helps inmate mothers "learn how to be better mothers by improving their parenting skills. This course focuses on issues of positive behavior management, child development, moral development, discipline, and family communication."

The Washington Corrections Center for Women at Gig Harbor offers parenting classes through Tacoma Community College. During the Fiscal Year 1994/1995, instructors taught seventeen courses on such subjects as parenting techniques, child development, family finances, and parenting from a distance.

The Peanut Butter and Jelly Program (ImPACT) at the New Mexico Women's Correctional Facility at Grants provides education and counseling to inmates prior to their release. "This program is designed to ease the transition from prison to family life for the inmate and her loved ones. During the last year of incarceration, an inmate may elect to participate in this four-phase program. It includes: instruction; family education and support that prepares mothers to aid their new family member in adjusting; therapeutic visitation of the inmate with children and spouse in a secure and stimulating environment under therapeutic supervision; and follow-up support with the inmate and the family.

At the Dwight Correctional Center in Illinois, the Motherlove parenting classes consist of eight classes designed to cover a wide range of issues associated with appropriate parenting skills. Those mothers mandated by court order to participate are given first preference.

The following classes are available at the Topeka Correctional Facility in Kansas:

- parenting (taught by United Methodist Women volunteers)
- effective black parenting (sponsored by the Shawnee Regional Prevention Center and taught by trained volunteers)
- preparing for the drug-free years (sponsored by the Shawnee Regional Prevention Center and the Kansas National Guard and taught by trained inmate facilitators)
- nutrition (sponsored by the Shawnee County Extension Office division of Kansas State University and taught by a nutrition assistant)
- crafts (sponsored and taught by United Methodist Women volunteers)

The following parenting classes are currently offered at the State Correctional Institution at Cambridge Springs, Pennsylvania: Basic Parenting I and II, child psychology/development, and parenting and recovery ("an eight-week course designed to help mothers who are in recovery from active drug addiction to develop skills as parents while still keeping their recovery in focus").

Parenting classes at the Mabel Bassett Correctional Center in Oklahoma City are sponsored by the public school system; the facility's medical unit provides classes for expectant mothers; and the county extension program offers classes on nutrition.

The Indiana Women's Prison in Indianapolis offers several components in their parenting program:

- the YWCA Incarcerated Mothers Program provides courses that focus on family and parenting issues. The Parents in Touch Program provides monthly meetings of mothers, and encourages communication between mothers and their children; mothers mail home individualized twelve-month "Caring Calendars" to their children so that each month mothers make a craft item to send to their children along with a letter to place in that month's pocket.

- mothers can participate in various support groups that deal with a variety of issues.

The warden of the Federal Correctional Institution at Danbury, Connecticut, Charles Stewart, Jr., writes (January 19, 1996):

> The Parenting Program provides solutions to issues women and children encounter when mothers are incarcerated. It teaches inmate mothers coping skills, how to interpret their children's behavior, how to administer positive discipline, and how to give direction from a distance. The program stresses the importance of developing healthy relationships with their family as well as with the caretakers of the children. Most important, the inmate mothers are able to practice, demonstrate, and apply what is learned with their children.

This institution offers classes in anger management, mother-child communication, creative parenting, family literacy education, skills for family support, substance abuse education, prenatal care/baby's health and parenting, and others. There is also a Parents Anonymous support group. The classes and programs are also provided in Spanish for the non-English proficient inmates.

The Federal Prison Camp at Bryan, Texas "has a parenting program which teaches its inmates numerous parenting skills and techniques. The program was recently recognized as one of the best of Texas."

Child Rearing Attitudes of Incarcerated Parents

Slagle (1981) conducted a study of child-rearing attitudes of thirty incarcerated parents and concluded:

> Parenting programs in and of themselves are not sufficient to promote feelings of parental worth and positive attitudes toward children . . . Parenting programs may serve to educate mothers about reciprocal interactions but other programs must also be available to promote positive growth experiences, such as educational advancement, vocational training, and support groups.

A similar conclusion was reached by LeFlore and Holston (1989). In their evaluation of parenting classes at the women's institution in Mississippi, they compared the attitudes toward parenting of inmate mothers with a matched control group of nonincarcerated mothers and found no statistically significant difference. This study emphasized that the incarcerated mothers needed help in achieving their goals of positive parenting. They concluded that vocational training and follow-up job placement assistance were needed for successful parole.

Parenting Programs at Boot Camps

(The following information is from Cheryl L. Clark's article "Sisters Are Doing It for Themselves" in *Juvenile and Adult Boot Camps* (American Correctional Association 1996).

> The majority of women participating in boot camp programs are mothers. In general, they are raising their children alone, without the children's fathers to assist and support them. Given their history of abuse, it is almost inevitable that their parenting skills are poor, and that they have perpetuated the cycle of neglect and abuse with their own children which they learned when they were children themselves. This cycle has been discussed repeatedly in research about child abuse, domestic violence, and other issues contributing to dysfunction. . . .
>
> All "abusive parents had themselves been abused as children. There were no exceptions. Since the majority of women in corrections by their own admission have been abused, teaching them parenting skills is critical to working effectively with these women.

Most often they have had children either because they did not know how to protect themselves from unwanted pregnancies or because they wanted someone to love them and a baby seemed the answer. Babies for many are like playing with dolls; they do not understand that the baby would have needs, too, and that they could not put the infant down when they were tired of playing. They have not been taught how to bathe, diaper, properly feed, and care for infants. Often, they do not know how to cope with their children when they cry, are upset, or sick. One young woman, horribly scared and mutilated by abuse in her past tearfully told how she and her sister accidentally had killed her baby when they were high and could not stop her crying. She was never charged with the crime, because they were homeless at the time it happened and the baby was an unknown. She could not remember what they had done with the baby, just that they 'got rid of it.'

These types of stories are far too usual among women in corrections. Parenting skills are critically needed. Any boot camp program for women must focus on parenting, and issues of abuse and domestic violence. Health and nutrition are equally important. Most women have badly neglected their health and are very likely to have sexually transmitted diseases, neglected themselves during their pregnancies and be HIV positive. They are out of shape and physically weak. Many are either overweight or malnourished from neglect and poor nutrition and do not know how to take care of themselves.

In general, they are babies of babies. It is not unusual for a seventeen-to-nineteen year old to have more than one child, living with a thirty-two-year-old grandmother. Indeed, many of the women, less than thirty-five years old in Shock . . . are grandmothers, themselves. Preparing these young women to be good parents to their children is an important contribution for boot camps to offer.

One approach to parenting skills in Shock [Boot Camps] is the children's reading program. We developed this to teach mothers and fathers how to select books appropriate for reading to their children. There is a children's book corner in the prison library and children's stories are used to reinforce some of the concepts we teach in the program. . . . Many of these young women missed having stories read to them as children and are excited by the whole new world opening up to them.

Furloughs

Of the eighty-six institutions contacted for this study, only 50 percent provided furloughs for inmates to spend time with their families and children, in addition to emergency furloughs. "Mother release" or furlough programs for mothers to be with their children are recommended by a number of writers (McCarthy 1979; McGowan and Blumenthal 1978; Palme 1972; Sametz 1980; Stanton 1980).

Nigel Walker (1992), in writing about "home leaves," the British equivalent of furloughs, points out that if their purpose is to "maintain" links with the family, they should be granted soon after the offender is sent to prison and at regular intervals. The practice of making them available only when prisoners are nearing the time of their release is more in keeping with a goal of "renewing" family relationships. This is certainly as true of American prison policies as it is of British.

Walker describes the policies in Sweden, where "'regular short-term home leave is normally granted after a short qualifying period," and where even lifers are "allowed leave in the third year of sentence." After describing some of the problems to be expected with such policies, Walker suggests we study how Sweden has managed to solve them. He concludes:

> If "maintaining links with families is" meant to be more than mere lip-service . . . [granting] regular home leaves at an early stage in a prisoner's sentence would be more effective than any conceivable improvement in facilities for family visits to prisons.

At Bedford Hills Correctional Center in New York, inmate mothers are able to spend a furlough week with their children at Providence House in Brooklyn. McCarthy (1979 1980) described the furlough programs in New York and Connecticut, concluding furlough programs ease the time remaining on the inmate's sentence. While the furloughs may preserve mother-child ties, they may not prepare the inmate mother for assumption of parental responsibilities. The home visit may not be devoted to parenting but to visiting with friends and relatives and sharing activities with their children (McCarthy 1980).

In addition, Bedford Hills has a furlough program administered by the New York State Department of Correctional Services. "This program allows statutorily eligible inmates to furlough to an approved residence for a period of up to seven days. Inmates must be within two years of their earliest release and not be convicted of a violent felony offense. Additional factors which are considered in making an eligibility determination are disciplinary adjustment, program history, active warrants, and physical and mental health" (letter of Joseph T. Smith, Deputy Superintendent for Program Services, January 24, 1996).

In California, work furlough programs are available to every incarcerated woman. This is a volunteer program that involves specific eligibility requirements. The community facilities (Community Prisoners Mother Program) also approve leave requests for work, education, training, family visitation, medical and dental appointments, and other discretionary reasons.

In Florida, at the Forest Hills Unit at Lowell and Levy Forestry Camp, a pregnancy furlough may be granted when an approved inmate is within the last trimester of her pregnancy. In Georgia, a pregnant inmate may be granted a "parole reprieve" of six to eight weeks in order to give birth and arrange for the placement of her infant.

In Pennsylvania, at the State Correctional Institution at Muncy:

> inmates who meet the minimum standards for pre-release status (one-half of a minimum sentence served, nine months with a good conduct record, and nine months on institution grounds) are eligible to participate in furloughs nine months prior to their minimum release date.

At the Women's Community Correctional Center in Kailua, Hawaii, the women are eligible for three types of furloughs: resocialization furloughs, work furloughs, and extended furloughs (comparable to what is work release in other facilities). Women who may be on the verge of being revoked from extended furloughs may be sent to the Day Reporting Program for assistance in life-skills or for substance-abuse treatment.

In Kansas, at the Topeka Correctional Facility, minimum custody, nonviolent men and women who are eligible for parole within twelve months may be granted two- through five-day furloughs.

The Baltimore Pre-Release Unit provides furloughs for men or women who are within nine months of a definite release date. These family leaves gradually increase from twelve hours to forty-eight hours away from the facility.

The New Mexico Women's Correctional Facility at Grants allows regular furloughs:

> every sixty days to minimum custody inmates who have been incarcerated at least one year. Furloughs are granted to eligible inmates to visit family, to visit a seriously ill member of her immediate family, to attend the funeral of an immediate family member, to obtain medical services not otherwise available, or to establish a release program prior to parole or discharge. Furloughs do not exceed seventy-two hours.

The Iowa Legislature introduced a "Work Release Law" (Chapter 220, Section 2) in 1967. Along with the usual provisions for work release and educational release, the statute authorized the following: "In the case of female inmates the program may include housekeeping in her domicile."

This section (Chapter 247A.2, Iowa Code of 1971) was amended in 1974 by Chapter 1093, "an Act relating to statutory provisions affecting the legal treatment of male and female persons." The amendment broadened the statute to apply to both sexes, as follows: "in the case of inmates who have children in their homes under the age of eighteen years, the program may include child care and housekeeping in their homes (247A.2)."

The Code of Iowa (1995) includes this provision for the Work Release Program (904.401): "An inmate may be placed on work release status in the inmate's own home, under appropriate circumstances, which may include child care and housekeeping in the inmate's own home." However, this type of work release status rarely, if ever, has been granted.

Prisons and Kids described Iowa as having a liberal furlough policy at the Iowa Correctional Institution for Women at Mitchellville; however, Cathy Pargo sued Iowa in 1992 (*Pargo et al. v. Elliott et al.*, U.S. Dist. Court, S.D., Iowa). She showed that during a three-year period, 592 male inmates were granted community furloughs from the Iowa Correctional Release Center at Newton, Iowa, but none of the women at the Iowa Correctional Institution for Women were granted such furloughs. (Several furloughs were granted to women after this lawsuit was filed.) The explanation by the warden was that the "female inmates are immediately paroled when they are close enough to release and are no longer subject to mandatory minimums." The Circuit Court of Appeals (eighth Circuit) found the warden's explanation credible, that is, by the time the women inmates meet "strict furlough criteria" they already have been released.

> In Canada:
> all inmates incarcerated in provincial correctional institutions have access to the Temporary Absence Program or parole. These programs provide inmates the opportunity to be released from custody for a specific period of time, to participate in community programs, maintain contact with the community and to assist in their reintegration into society.

Family and Conjugal Visits

The term "family visits" is sometimes preferred to "conjugal visits." The programs are similar in nature and are intended to preserve and maintain the marital bond and the family unit.

Eight states currently permit conjugal visits in women's institutions. These states are California, Connecticut, Maryland, Mississippi, New Jersey, New Mexico, New York, and Washington. The Canadian Prison for Women at Kingston, Ontario also allows conjugal visits. Although the percentage of institutions allowing conjugal visits has increased only slightly since 1985, the number of states (and provinces) allowing conjugal visits has increased from six to nine.

Each California penal institution operates a conjugal visiting program. However, the Community Prisoner Mother Program and the Family Foundations Program do not allow conjugal visits.

At the Connecticut Correctional Institution at Niantic, for selected long-term women inmates, twenty-eight-hour visits in a three-bedroom trailer are permitted every ninety days with family members (Glasser 1990). Family members may be spouses, parents, stepparents, children, grandparents, and

grandchildren . . . However, some inmate mothers have not been able to have visits with their children because there is no available caretaker who could supervise them on the visit (all children less than eighteen must be supervised by an adult during the visit).

The Washington Corrections Center for Women at Gig Harbor (formerly the Purdy Treatment Center for Women) has the Extended Family Visit program. (This pilot program was adopted and extended to the men's institution . . . an interesting example of the women's movement having a liberating impact on men).

> Initial visits under the program are for twenty-four hours and take place in a detached trailer. The visits are essentially unmonitored except for periodic institution counts. These normally take place five times per day. Subsequent extended family visits are forty-three hours in duration.

The purpose of the program is to enable inmates "to maintain close contact with immediate family members. This includes not only spouses and children, but also, parents, siblings, grandparents, and occasionally other close relatives." Of the ninety extended family visits that took place in 1995, in twenty-six cases, the visit was with a husband; in forty-two cases it was with the inmate's children. "The children may have been escorted by the father or some other adult family member. Sixty-two extended family visits included family members other than spouses and children."

Showalter and Jones (1980) have described marital workshops at the Kansas State Penitentiary at Lansing in which inmates within six months of their release are able to explore their marital relationship for an entire weekend.

At the Bedford Hills Correctional Facility in

New York, the Family Reunion Program "provides eligible inmates with the opportunity to spend two days in a modular housing unit with approved family members." A study of New York's Family Reunion Program was conducted based on interviews and standardized scales comparing thirty-three Family Reunion Program inmates and their wives with twenty-eight nonparticipating couples (Carlson and Cervera 1991). The sample was drawn from several unidentified facilities in New York. They found that scores on "cohesion" and "adaptability" were not statistically significant between the groups, and that the number of conjugal visits was not related to cohesion or closeness to their wives and children. This study did not attempt to relate conjugal visits to recidivism, although it cites other studies that show the maintenance of family ties is related to lower rates of recidivism.

The following nations also authorize conjugal visits, according to one survey (Goetting 1982b): Australia, Denmark, Finland, the Federal Republic of Germany, Iceland, India, Iran, the Netherlands, Norway, Philippine Islands, the Soviet Union, Spain, Sweden, Switzerland, and Yugoslavia.

Latin America

In Latin America, fourteen countries allow conjugal visits: Bolivia, Brazil, Colombia, Costa Rica, Cuba, Ecuador, El Salvador, Guatemala, Honduras, Mexico, Nicaragua, Paraguay, Peru, and Venezuela (Goetting 1982a).

In Mexico, particularly at Las Islas Marias, "the reclusorios are in stark contrast with the fortress-like prisons in the United States" (Burke 1981, American Correctional Association 1981). The reclusorio is "visually attractive, quiet, tranquil, and like a college campus" with small one- or two-story buildings. Family visits are an integral part of prison life, with one-third of the compound designed for family activities. Conjugal visits are permitted in a motel-like building.

While United States' prisons emphasize the equality of all inmates, Mexican prisons do not attempt to remove individual and class differences. Inmates may keep almost anything in their rooms; dormitories have cooking facilities for preparing food from home; inmates wear their own clothing; and small shops sell "everything." Labor is not compulsory and prisoners can pursue their own profit-making endeavors or do nothing. A few cottages can be rented by wealthy inmates. One inmate "even has his secretary come in every day" (Burke 1981).

According to Wilkinson (1990, citing research by others), conjugal visiting results "in fewer acts of violence among inmates and a decrease in homosexual activity." In his study of a Mexican prison, Wilkinson reports that inmates are allowed to carry their own money and can buy almost anything that they can purchase on the outside, including radios, television sets, irons, clothes, arts and crafts materials, phone privileges, visits from families and friends, better sleeping facilities, and conjugal visits. If an inmate is disruptive, he or she loses these privileges and is not allowed to purchase them.

Guatemala has been referred to as having the "most extreme form of familism" in men's prisons of all the American nations, but its women's prison, Santa Teresa, prohibits conjugal visiting (Goetting 1984). At the Granja Modelo Rehabilitacione Pavon, the largest prison for men with more than 2,000 inmates, there is a freedom of movement that is not found in most United States' prisons. Walkways are lined with restaurants and craft shops operated by inmates and their families. The crafts include "jewelry of seeds, bone, stones, silver and nuts, macrame, pottery, weaving, crocheting, leatherwork, and woodwork."

Other products made are "neckties, earrings, plant hangers, pocketbooks, belts, hammocks, soccer balls, baskets, and furniture."

Goetting writes:

> This emphasis on familism which permeates both policy and atmosphere at Pavon reflects the assumption that both familial continuity and privacy are part of the inherent rights of every human being. The pervasive attitude regarding visitation is not one of privilege or of liberalism. Family visitations are not something which the establishment uses to stimulate incentive for good behavior or yields to under pressures of human rights. Instead it is viewed as a manifestation of life's natural order not to be interfered with because of incarceration (1984).

Conjugal Visits in the United States

The earliest programs for conjugal visiting in the United States were established in the late nineteenth and early twentieth centuries in South Carolina and Mississippi. Originally available only to males, they were subsequently extended to female inmates. At the Mississippi State Penitentiary at Parchman, eligibility for participation is restricted to legally married spouses. There are no restrictions based on the nature of the crime for which the inmate is imprisoned, nor for disciplinary reasons. Private visits at the institutions have been authorized in houses, efficiency apartments, tents, trailers, mobile homes, and cars. Various eligibility requirements and policies are detailed by Goetting (1982a). The visitors typically are legal spouses, children, parents and grandparents, siblings, and legal guardians.

The Debate on Conjugal Visits

In summarizing the arguments in the debate about conjugal association, Goetting (1982a, 1982c) identifies the opposing factions as the conservatives, the correctional establishment, and right-wing politicians. She identifies the advocates of conjugal visiting programs as liberal social scientists, journalists, and ex-inmates. The arguments of both factions, she says, are the "same as thirty-five years ago" and cover moral, practical, and legal issues. They run as follows:

Opposition to conjugal visits. From a moral standpoint, opponents cite blatant inequity favoring married inmates, or a transformation of prisons into "whorehouses" corrupting staff and degrading inmates' wives. From a practical perspective, opponents contend: there is public opposition (although opinion surveys report 50 percent of the public support conjugal association in correctional institutions); custody and security problems may occur; programs may cost too much; and the wives will become pregnant and produce children who will have to be supported by public assistance. From the legal perspective, opponents argue: there may be liability risks to prisons; and people signing waivers may not understand their significance, so they may be unenforceable.

In favor of conjugal visits. From a moral perspective, supporters appeal to humanism; emphasize the sexual and emotional frustrations of the inmate and his or her "innocent" spouse; and cite the emotional support provided by human intimacy and its enhancement of an inmate's self-esteem.

From a practical perspective, advocates argue that conjugal visits: reduce tension and hostility among inmates; provide an incentive for conformity and enhance the institutional objective of "control"; promote a normal lifestyle in preparation for transition and reintegration into a free society; increase the likelihood of postrelease success; foster marital stability; and reduce homosexuality and rapes. Regarding this last issue, Goetting comments, "Much evidence suggests that prison homosexuality is instead an expression of the urge for mastery by people who have been placed in a position of powerlessness, a condition not solely related to sexual deprivation."

From a legal perspective, supporters contend the denial of conjugal visits may be unconstitutional based on the first, eighth, and fourteenth amendments. There is a possibility for marital and inmate stress developing as a result of family visitation and conjugal association programs (Goetting 1984). She recommends that policymakers should address the potential problem through a combination of stress reduction and counseling in stress management. She concludes (1982a):

> Family visitation programs in the United States undoubtedly provide a more humane institutional environment for inmates but such practices cannot at this time be based without question on other alleged advantages. There is no solid research support for contentions that such programs reduce homosexuality, enhance social control, normalize prison lifestyle, increase postrelease success, or stabilize marriages. At the same time, there is clear evidence of security and operational problems. Research exploring the outcomes of private family visiting is badly needed to aid administrators in decisions about the implementation of new programs and improvement of those already in operation.

Bates (1989) has summarized some of the arguments in favor and opposed to conjugal visits, but he adds a new incentive: the AIDS crisis. He argues that:

> with the probability that AIDS is being spread among inmates in even the best-managed correctional system, the door is left open for inmates to allege a constitutional right to a conjugal visit based on their fear of living in an environment where the risk of contracting AIDS is great. Indeed, there have to date been several suits brought by inmates seeking protection from those in the prison population with AIDS.

Bates admits that the idea of conjugal visits reducing the risk of AIDS is untested, and he also calls attention to the long-term implications of using conjugal visits to combat AIDS. For example, would single inmates want access to conjugal visits under the equal protection argument?

Community Facilities

Seventeen states (compared to five states in 1985) report that they have community facilities for mothers and their children at various stages in the mothers' incarceration (please see Resources for these states).

Community residential facilities have greater benefits and fewer drawbacks than prison nurseries (Deck 1988). Among the benefits of community residential facilities are the following: they are cost effective; they are in the best interests of the child; they are rehabilitative for the mother; they reduce prison crowding; there is a minimal loss of protection to the public; and recidivism rates are reduced as a result of the maintenance of family ties.

The Women's Residential Correctional Facility in Des Moines, Iowa was opened in June 1993, and the "Women with Children" wing was opened in May 1994. The facility houses forty-eight women, including eight mothers and up to twelve children under the age of five years. Pregnant women may be admitted to the facility and remain with their infants. This is a privately contracted facility with oversight by the Fifth Judicial District. Residents include women sentenced by the court to probation or as a result of a probation or parole revocation hearing; those under federal jurisdiction; jail transfers; those serving sentences for a third offense of operating a vehicle while intoxicated; work releases; and pretrial detainees. Women may be transferred to this facility for work release or parole from the Iowa Correctional Institution for Women at Mitchellville. Residents are required to pay weekly rent, obtain employment, and participate in treatment programming. Each resident has a case counselor and a substance abuse counselor. If needed, referrals may be made to community agencies and programs.

As mentioned earlier, California has some experience with community facilities for mothers and their children. In the initial legislation, eligible inmates were those who:

- will probably be released within two years (later changed to six years)
- have no prior prison term
- have been the infant's primary caretaker prior to incarceration
- have a child young enough so that by the end of the mother's sentence the child is not older than two (later changed to six) years
- have not been found unfit by the court
- have not had more than thirty days elapse between incarceration and application date

In addition, the California Department of Corrections established rules regarding exclusion from the program. They are based on the inmate mother's institutional behavior. The mother would not be eligible if she were guilty of the use or possession of narcotics, were violent or assaultive toward the staff or other inmates, in need of lockup, or unwilling to become constructively involved in treatment programs while in the institution.

The revised statute requires only that the inmate mother has less than six years left in her sentence; was the primary caretaker of the infant prior to incarceration; was not found unfit by the court; and has made an application within thirty days of her incarceration. Placement of the program under the Parole and Community Services division, however, has resulted in one of the criticisms of the current statute; that the inmate mother in a community facility with her child technically still is in prison. Although special seventy-two-hour leave is granted, the mother is restricted in her movements at the facility. Thus, she is prohibited from assuming full parental responsibilities.

The Prisoner Mother-Infant Program in Salinas, California is located in the Helen McCaig House. This is a six-bedroom house that serves as a community-based correction center operated under contract between the California Department of Corrections and "Friends Outside," a national nonprofit organization with fifteen chapters. Incarcerated mothers may apply to reside at the house with their child while serving their term of commitment. A resident is able to learn parenting skills, participate in substance abuse treatment programs, attend school, learn vocational skills, and gain employment experience.

Roulet *et al.* (1993) describes Providence House V in Brooklyn as a residential facility for mothers paroled from the Bedford Hills Correctional Facility and their children. Each of eight Providence Houses is managed by a former Bedford inmate. The parolees are able to seek employment and permanent housing while they live there. In addition, "My Mother's House" is a foster home run by St. Joseph's Family Services. "Its purpose is to house the children of inmates who have no family members to care for them while their mothers are incarcerated."

In Massachusetts, incarcerated mothers nearing release are transferred to the prerelease center at Lancaster (near Boston) where eligible mothers are permitted to have overnight and weekend visits with their children in house trailers. This program "provides a more natural setting for visits thus lessening the stress caused to children and their parents by incarceration, and serv[ing] to better prepare mothers to resume day-to-day responsibility for taking care of their children" (Jamison 1984).

The State Correctional Institution at Muncy, Pennsylvania "recently started a relationship with Hutchinson Place, which is a Philadelphia-based program designed to house inmates and their preschool children. The purpose is to reunite mothers and their children in the community prior to parole."

The Federal Prison Camp at Bryan, Texas has a program called "Mothers and Infants Together." This program is "a community placement for pregnant inmates to deliver the child and reside with the child after its birth for up to ninety days."

Visitation Policies

Thirty-one of eighty-six institutions (in twenty-one states and the provinces of Ontario and Manitoba) allow children of incarcerated mothers to have overnight stays at the institutions (see Table 1). Breen (1995b) describes the benefits of visitation programs and concludes, the visitation program "can be a bridge that allows the child to move between two very different worlds and to adapt to the challenges of both. It can play a major role in the lives of these children—the real victims of crime in America."

Visitation policies and conditions vary considerably at each prison (Baunach 1982). In one study (Neto and Bainer 1982), 78 percent of forty state prisons surveyed had traditional visitation policies of fixed hours, searches, and contact visits, and 60 percent provided play areas for children. Only one prison did not permit contact.

According to Fuller (1993), in recent years, budgetary constraints and corrections' priorities in some prisons in California have resulted in visiting days being reduced from five days to two days a week. Before 1972, there were no visitation services available for persons visiting California state prisons. "In 1983, Assembly Bill No. 1512 was passed, requiring that the Department of Corrections establish and operate through a nonprofit agency a visitation center outside each adult state prison in California." Centerforce, Inc., a nonprofit agency founded in 1972, was awarded the contract by the Department of Corrections to operate these centers. Breen (1995a) describes some of the legislative efforts that resulted in this program. Each center provides the following:

- assistance to visitors with transportation between public transit terminals and prisons
- child care for visitors' children
- emergency clothing
- information on visiting regulations and processes
- referral to other agencies and services
- a sheltered area, which is outside of the security perimeter, for visitors who are waiting before and after visits

The Las Comadres program operates in each of California's women's prisons. It assists incarcerated mothers in the private, temporary placement of their children in foster homes during their prison terms. The program enables the mothers and their children to maintain their ties through frequent visits during the regularly scheduled institutional visiting hours. The program also provides parenting classes, which include health care, nutrition, self-esteem, and parenting skills. Staff also provide training and consultation in parenting issues and child care, and offer ongo-

ing support to both the inmate mother and the foster family.

"Camp Celebration" has been in operation at the Dwight Correctional Center at Dwight, Illinois. Stumbo and Little (1990), in their evaluation of Camp Celebration, list sixteen parenting programs at this institution. Fourteen of these programs were started in 1982 or more recently. The programs provide legal assistance, family advocacy, college courses, leadership training, transportation for children from the Chicago area, conflict resolution, and substance-abuse intervention. For the first three years it received federal funds; since then, it has continued to operate without federal assistance. There is a weekend camping experience on the grounds of the facility where mothers can spend forty-eight hours with their children. During thirteen weekends each summer, twelve mothers each weekend can spend time with their children (up to age sixteen) and are able to camp in four-person tents, sleep in sleeping bags, play games, and enjoy other activities designed to "help reunify families." Two of the main problems encountered are securing transportation for the children and obtaining permission from the children's caregivers. There have been no security problems (Stumbo and Little 1991).

At the Lancaster Pre-Release Center in Massachusetts, two house trailers (with three bedrooms each) are available for overnight visits between the mothers and their children.

Project REACH (Responsibility, Empowerment, Achievement, Coping Skills, and Healthy Relationships) is a program for incarcerated mothers, their families, and their children at the Metro Correctional Institution at Atlanta, Georgia that was initiated in 1981. In 1985, Georgia College in Milledgeville agreed to provide administrative and educational services. REACH has six primary components: parenting classes or groups; a family visitation program; monthly meetings of committed spouses and partners; resource office and clearinghouse; coordination of relevant programs; and additional services, including continuing education, transportation network, and legal services.

The Topeka Correctional Facility in Kansas allows minimum custody mothers completing a ten-hour parenting course to have a forty-eight-hour retreat with their children who are less than seventeen years of age. The retreats are sponsored by the United Methodist Women four times a year. Also, there are nine individual rooms with homelike furnishings at the facility for medium/minimum custody women to visit with their children on weekends from 8:00 A.M. to 3:30 P.M. There are similar areas available at the women's maximum custody unit, and the minimum custody men's unit.

The New Mexico Women's Correctional Facility at Grants allows family visits:

> between eligible inmates and their family in order to promote family stability and enhance the reintegration process. The visits range in length from six to twenty-four hours. An inmate must meet certain criteria to advance to a longer visit. Inmates who are furlough eligible may not participate in family visits.

Sack and Seidler (1978) interviewed twenty-two children visiting their fathers at the Oregon State Penitentiary in Salem, Oregon. They found that although the children placed a high value on their visits with their fathers, they also expressed conflicted feelings. The authors called for more research and the evaluation of new programs.

The Children's Visitation Program at the Huron Valley Correctional Facility in Michigan was subsequently moved to the Scott Correctional Facility in Plymouth, Michigan when the women inmates were transferred to that institution (Jose-Kampfner 1991). The program, which began in 1988, served not only to restore the bonds between mothers and children, but also to improve discipline at the institution. The visits between mothers and their children last about three hours on a Saturday once a month. Jose-Kampfner notes:

> children's visitation programs can be put in place in prisons at almost no cost. They must, however, involve the inmates, the institution, and the community.

At the Minnesota Correctional Facility at Shakopee, there are several visiting programs. Mothers with children under twelve-years old may have one child at a time spend Friday night and Saturday; these visits take place on all but one weekend each month. The Independent Living Unit allows greater independence of the mothers, and children may spend an entire weekend; however, only one mother in the four-inmate apartment can have her children at one time. For mothers with children between the ages of twelve to eighteen, a Parenting Teens Support group was organized in November 1994, at the suggestion of several inmates. After attending five meetings, the mothers and their teens are able to spend a Teen Day in a less formal setting than the visiting room, play games in the gym, and take part in other activities. There is also an Odyssey Group for long-term inmates that enables family members to have a meal with these inmates two times a year.

The North Carolina Correctional Institution for Women in Raleigh has a "Long Termers' Family Day" that is designed to "enhance family support of the long-term offender." Twice a year, families are encouraged to bring a meal and spend the day with the long-termer; this is offered in addition to the regularly scheduled weekly visitation.

The M.O.L.D. (Mother Offspring Life Development) program at the Nebraska Center for Women at York allows children to stay in their mothers' room for five days on a monthly basis. Overnight visits are limited to girls up to the age of twelve, and boys up to the age of nine. The children must be at least six months old and a mother is limited to two children. During the visit, an inmate mother is relieved of work assignments but is responsible for the activities and care of the children. Overnight visits are denied if an inmate is being disciplined by a restriction to her room.

At the Children's Center at the Bedford Hills Correctional Center in New York, overnight visits of children are made possible through the help of host families in the community. This program was started in 1980. During the summer, a child may spend one week with a host family and the child is brought to the Children's Center each morning to spend the day with his or her mother until 3:30 P.M. Because of the popularity of this program, it was expanded to the school year, and children arrive on Saturday, spend the night with a host family, and return to the institution on Sunday to visit their mother until they are transported by the Children's Center bus back to New York City in the afternoon.

P.A.C.T. Inc. (Parent and Child Together) is a nonprofit organization that began at the Federal Correctional Institution in Fort Worth,

Texas in 1984. "Since 1987, P.A.C.T. has worked primarily with an all-male inmate population." The program at Fort Worth "remains the only parent/child program of its kind in an all-male institution in the federal prison system" (Key 1993).

P.A.C.T. developed S.K.I.P. (Support for Kids with Incarcerated Parents) in 1987. This program consists of support groups for children during visitations. The curriculum consists of thirty lesson plans addressing five problem areas (Key 1993):

- self-esteem (developing respect for self)
- family relationships (developing respect for others)
- decision making (understanding choices and consequences)
- substance abuse (coping with a family member who is a substance abuser)
- prison life (coping with a parent in prison)

The P.A.C.T. program at the Springfield State Prison at Springfield, South Dakota, provides for an inmate mother and her children to spend a weekend every month at the institution. "The purpose of the program is to create a better understanding of the parental role, to provide the opportunity for the inmate mother to maintain some responsibility for the care of her child(ren) and to alleviate some of the stress experienced by both mother and child(ren) associated with the mother's incarceration."

From 1978 until 1994, women incarcerated at the Correctional Institution in Clinton, New Jersey, were able to spend weekends with their children at nearby Camp Tecumseh, a Salvation Army camp (Beavers-Luteran 1983, Driscoll 1985). The mothers, children, and staff were all involved in planning activities, including arts, crafts, discussion groups, and recreation. However, the use of the facility was donated to the program and when the Salvation Army proposed a fee for its use, the program was discontinued for lack of funding. In its place, at the institution there are currently a Mother/Child visitation program and the Girl Scout's Beyond Bars program.

The State Correctional Institution at Muncy, Pennsylvania has a mother-child retreat sponsored by the Salvation Army. In addition, local Mennonite families open their homes to the relatives of inmates so that the family members can visit the prison on several successive days (Couturier 1995).

The Renz Correctional Center in Jefferson City, Missouri has Agape House available to the families of inmates. Families can spend the night there while visiting inmates.

The Proceedings (1993), describe four hospitality homes in Canada that assist the families who are visiting prisoners or who wish to relocate to be near a loved one. These include: the John Howard Society Family House in Abbotsford, British Columbia (established in April 1984); Good Shepherd Hospitality House in Port Cartier, Quebec (since 1988); Springhouse in Springhill, Nova Scotia (opened in November 1985); and Bridge House in Kingston, Ontario.

In Montreal, Quebec, the Continuite-Famille Aupres des Detenues was founded in 1985 (Trepanier 1993). Its primary goal is "to allow incarcerated mothers to be in contact with their children in a stable and regular way in a site of their choice." The program offers parenting skills training, discussion groups, and celebrations of family occasions. There are two aspects to this program: the "Inside" program allows incarcerated mothers and their children to have supervised visits in a mobile home at Tanguay Prison; the "Outside" program is for ex-offenders.

The Mabel Bassett Correctional Center in Oklahoma City, Oklahoma has CAMP (Children and Mother's Program), which permit overnight visits two or three times a year. "Dues are $5.00 per child per quarter." An "additional fee is charged for overnights."

Support Services

There is a need for greater integration of supportive and social services that various governmental agencies provide to inmates and their children and families (Balasco-Barr 1995, Immarigeon 1994, Chesney-Lind and Immarigeon 1995, Chaiklin 1972; Henriques 1982, McGowan and Blumenthal 1978).

Gaudin (1984) has described a variety of roles for social workers working with incarcerated mothers and offers a model for practice. The model is intended to reduce the obstacles to the maintenance of mother-child relationships. Social worker roles are suggested to deal with dysfunctions on three levels:

Macro System Roles: To deal with dysfunctions at the state and national government levels, social workers can engage in efforts to change state laws on sentencing and sentencing alternatives, educate the community to alter punitive public attitudes, and work to locate prisons near population centers, as examples.

Mezzo System Roles: The efforts should be directed at changing dysfunctional organizational policies, practices, and procedures in prisons, social agencies, and law enforcement agencies. Examples would include efforts at correctional facilities to develop more liberal furlough policies and telephone privileges, improve the setting for visits, establish children's centers, and collect information on the needs of mothers in prisons. Other efforts could include establishing relationships with child welfare workers, workshops with police departments on handling the arrest of mothers with young children, and obtaining facts that might modify child-care placements and practices that obstruct mother-child relationships.

Micro System Roles: Gaudin describes efforts that can be made by social workers to improve the functioning of the incarcerated mothers, their children, and their extended families or other substitute child care providers. These activities would include the counseling of mothers, teaching them coping mechanisms, and preventing damage to the children "by achieving changes in laws, sentencing practices, and organizational policies and procedures that bring about and maintain the separation of inmate mothers and their children."

Legal services often are required by inmates with custody problems as well as for handling appeals and other issues related to their current offense and conviction. Discussion groups are another needed support for inmates in addition to individual counseling. Parents Anonymous is a self-help group that addresses child-abuse problems, and it has been used in various institutions. Clement (1993) describes thirty-eight chapters of Parents Anonymous in Virginia alone. Substance abuse problems also frequently are treated in discussion/therapy groups.

Clement concludes her survey of programs for incarcerated women in this way: "In light

of the inadequate support of the general public through the Department of Corrections, the fact that there are programs for females is a testimony to the private and other public agencies, through dedicated staff, who have developed programs to meet these needs."

At the State Correctional Institution at Cambridge Springs, Pennsylvania, "one-on-one counseling with inmates who are trying to establish or reestablish relationships with their children" is offered, according to Martha K. Miller, the Director of the Parenting Program, "WINGS for Kids" (Women Inside Needing Guidance and Support) (letter of January 24, 1996):

> We deal with women daily trying to locate their children, talking with their child's school teachers/counselors, discussing progress with caseworkers and dealing with hospitals. We're finding that many of the children left behind are in need of professional help. We offer the inmates directories of resources in the children's home communities so that the moms and the children's caregivers can decide on the help that the children need. The inmate mother, working with the child's caregiver, can coordinate help for the child from prison. The inmate mothers can and do take part in their child's counseling and progress by being available, by phone, to the child's therapist. This seems to alleviate some of the ongoing pressures the child and mother must face during their separation. The end result is to have a happier and healthier reunification between the mom and children as well as to cut down on mother's likelihood for recommitting.

The WINAS program (Women In Need of Alternate Solutions) at the Massachusetts Correctional Institution at Framingham provides education and treatment for inmates who have a history of and/or are at risk for abusing children. The goal of the WINAS program is to teach inmates to develop alternative strategies for managing their violent behavior, and it is anticipated that this will decrease family violence within the home. The program has the following components:

In phase I, the group focuses on teaching inmates appropriate behaviors as an alternative to aggressive, assaultive and other inappropriate behaviors. In phase II, the group focuses more in depth on the issues raised in phase I and is "skills based." The inmates are also required to participate in Parents Anonymous. This support group relies on a volunteer from the community.

At the State Correctional Institution at Muncy, Pennsylvania, therapeutic services are "targeted on all aspects of abuse, including domestic violence, sexual assault victims, and incest survivors. This year marks the opening of a housing unit with a therapeutic community setting designed for inmates participating in intensive abuse therapy."

The Columbia River Correctional Institution in Portland, Oregon, has an "intensive residential alcohol and drug treatment" program, "Turning Point," for fifty males and fifty females. The program is provided under a contract with ASAP Treatment Services, Inc. in Portland.

> A father or mother at level four of the program may request and present a plan for his or her child to be allowed to come to the Columbia River Correctional Institution for an incrementally increased visitation schedule, up to eight hours. There is a room with age-appropriate equipment and toys in which the child or children may visit. A planned schedule may include using the kitchen or main room of each treatment unit as well. The idea is to maintain the parental bond with the child while the inmate is incarcerated.
>
> Also, Women In Community Service (WISC) is a national program for women, most usually offered in Job Corps. There is a mentorship component to the program, and it has made a difference in the female prisoners' lives in Oregon. The program consists of eight weeks of life skills classes taught by volunteers from the

community, and assignment of a mentor who guides them through the transition back to the community. Life skills' participants learn to improve their self-esteem and implement a life action plan by developing skills in assertiveness, self-advocacy, child management, money management, employability, and coping with crises. Since the program's inception in 1991, 207 WICS graduates have been released from Columbia River Correctional Institution. At the twelve-month point, only 10.7 percent have returned. This rate of recidivism is far below state averages. The cost of keeping a woman in prison has been estimated to be $20,000 per year compared to the lifeskills training investment of $1,000 per student (communication from Barbara Mealey, Program Services Manager, April 25, 1996).

Another advocacy organization is the Osborne Association, a nonprofit criminal justice organization founded in 1933. It offers a broad spectrum of programs in New York State institutions, as well as Alternatives to Incarceration (ATI) programs for parolees, probationers, ex-offenders and their families, and substance abusers. FamilyWorks was founded in 1986 and is helping rebuild family ties broken during a father's incarceration. Living-Well was started in 1991 for HIV positive parolees; it also provides education for parole officers about the needs of HIV positive clients. El Rio is a drug free treatment program that was started in 1990 as an alternative to incarceration for probationers and parolees in New York City.

The Oregon Women's Correctional Center in Salem has a program, "Recovery In Focus," that is presented "with the cooperation of the Tualatin Valley Mental Health Center." The program is a six-month prerelease substance abuse treatment program. The goals of the program are "to promote treatment and recovery, prevent recidivism, relapse and homelessness, and to reunite women with their children." The parenting component of the program is divided into three parts: instructions and discussion, family therapy, and release planning.

In Canada, at the Portage Correctional Institution for Women, in Portage la Prairie, Manitoba, case managers focus on the needs of the residents. "They set up individualized programs with each resident to address those needs and to develop a smooth transition between incarceration and release to the community. This program has been operating since 1982." Many residents are given "meaningful work activities through the use of community placements" which allow for "increased contact between the resident, the institution, and citizens in the community." In addition to church services and bible studies,

> instruction in native culture and spiritual values is provided each week by a native elder, who also visits the institution on a biweekly basis to offer individual counseling to residents. Feast days and traditional ceremonies are held in the institution. Visiting elders and speakers on native culture are frequent. A native advisory board was established in 1990, with members from the native community as well as staff from the institution. A sweat lodge was constructed in 1991 in cooperation with Agassiz Centre for Youth.

Morin (1993) describes a program in Montreal, Quebec that is intended for the dysfunctional family. The director of the program states:

> The family plays a key role in supporting the reintegration of inmates and former inmates into society. However, in working with these clients, we find that the family is often at the core of a set of problems, the result of a dysfunction dating from before their incarceration. Clients who have a dysfunctional family background marked by crime, alcoholism, drugs or violence will find the same family there when they are released. In such cases,

the family may even tip the scales in favour of failure during reintegration.

Citing John Bradshaw (*Family Secrets: What You Don't Know Can Hurt You*. New York: Bantam. 1995) on the dysfunctional family and employing William Glasser's Reality Therapy, this program helps clients to break free of, or step back from their family; to create their own family unit, as they want it to be; to no longer allow their family to interfere in their life; and to define their own identity and what they want to make of their life.

Transportation is another needed support service. Inmates whose children are temporarily placed in foster homes are often concerned about maintaining contact with the foster parents (Buckles and LaFazia 1973). If the children are in a foster home near the institution, maintaining communication and scheduling regular visits are obviously easier than if the child is at a great distance from the institution. In the latter case, transportation problems sometimes have been overcome with help from volunteer organizations such as Prison Fellowship and Parents Anonymous. Special social service personnel may be used. For example, foster parents may be reluctant to spend time and money to bring the children to visit their inmate parents, or they may be opposed to maintaining such contacts. In these cases, the institution may employ a coordinator to function as a liaison between the parent and the foster family or child welfare agency.

Barry *et al.* (1995) recommends that children of incarcerated parents be placed in foster homes as near to the institution as possible. Hungerford (1993) in his research on inmate mothers, their children, and their caregivers recommends a greater use of community-based correctional programs; greater involvement of social service and child welfare personnel in providing assistance to incarcerated mothers and the caregivers of their children; and placing female inmates in prisons close to their children.

Penal Colonies

Probably no topic in this monograph is as controversial as prison colonies. The term alone awakens thoughts of Devil's Island or Franz Kafka. However, several writers have described positive and benign aspects of prison colonies. They are included here because they offer opportunities for parents and children to remain together.

Johnson (1990) has described the history and theory associated with penal colonies or open prisons, as well as given examples of their operation in various societies, particularly in Japan. Depending on the degree of constraint imposed on the inhabitants, there are similarities with other alternatives to prisons, such as, minimum security camps, therapeutic communities, halfway houses, residential facilities, home confinement, open prisons, unit management, open parole camps, minimum live-out units, borstals, rehabilitative aid hostels, and electronic monitoring. Although not the subject of Johnson's paper nor of this book, one could develop a continuum of alternatives that would include all of these possibilities.

Johnson describes the following opportunities for employment and vocational training that these institutions have provided training in: construction machinery, animal husbandry, metal-processing shops, scrap steel operations, pollution cleanup and environmental remediation, shipbuilding, equipment repair, airport construction, highway construction, lumber camps, remodeling and reconstruction projects, conservation projects, farming and forestry camps, and arc welding. If prison industries were included in this continuum, these areas of employment and training would be expanded considerably.

Prison colonies have been established in Brazil, Peru, India, Jordan, Mexico, the Philippines, and the Soviet Union (Cavan and Zemans 1958, Goetting 1982b, 1984). In the Philippines, 3,600 minimum-security prisoners and their families may serve the remainder of their sentences in the Davao penal colony after completing one-fifth of their sentences. They are provided with plots of land, tools for farming, subsistence funds, clothing, and schooling for their children either within the colony or on the island.

In their conclusion, Cavan and Zemans (1958) refer to earlier recommendations regarding experimentation with home leave. They add "the tentative suggestion that some open prisons [in the United States] might like to experiment with the practice of permitting families of prisoners to live on the grounds." Thirty-eight years later, there are still no "open prisons" (to this author's knowledge) in the United States.

A Canadian publication referred to these as "limited access correctional communities" or LACCS (Zambrowsky 1984). In this article, the author does not take a positive or negative position but raises questions that need to be addressed. Which offenders would be eligible? Would families be willing to join offenders in such colonies? Would this be an unfair choice imposed upon the families of inmates? Is the government prepared to support such communities? Canadian officials responded: "Unfortunately, the program . . . is no longer being considered by the Ministry of the Solicitor General or the Correctional Service of Canada (Letter of May 7, 1996 from K. J. Wiseman, Assistant Commissioner, Correctional Service of Canada).

In *The Open Prison: Saving Their Lives and Our Money*, Chaneles (1973) advocates a broad range of reforms for corrections in the United States, including the establishment of "transitional communities," another euphemism for penal colonies. He cites several possibilities:

- Prisons could be converted into factories, schools, hospitals, and meeting places and could be merged with the surrounding communities.
- Transitional communities could be in or near large cities as expansions of factories or attached to colleges.
- Such communities could be created in the deserts or established in the abandoned coal-mining towns of Appalachia.

A Variety of Advantages

In "The Penal Colony: Relic or Reform?" Murton (1983a) argues convincingly for the benefits, including the low cost, of establishing domestic penal colonies in geographically dispersed areas based on the Civilian Conservation Corps model used in the United States during the depression and penal colonies in Mexico, India, and the Philippines. An innovative element is that civilian workers and their dependents voluntarily could commit themselves to these colonies.

He cites the following advantages (1983a and 1983b): Colonies would provide for the banishment of prisoners. Inmates could build their own facilities and, through self-government, would have a vested interest in making them livable. The colonies would be inexpensive to build and self-supporting; inmates could work on public works projects, which in turn would eliminate idleness. The costs of incarceration would be transferred from the victim to the offender. Inmates would be compensated financially, and therefore, would be able to make restitution payments and pay taxes. They would learn a trade and their family unit could be preserved. Another benefit, Murton says, is that inmates would learn responsibility by accepting responsibility for their crimes, their dependents, their incarceration and their obligation to society. Lastly, there would be less institutional violence, fewer incidents, escapes, and assaults, and an inmate's transition on release would be easier.

"You don't put a duck in a sandbox to teach him how to swim," says Murton (1983b) in arguing for a corrective environment that prepares inmates for the world to which they will return. "The evil of the penal colony was not inherent in the philosophy; it was a function of the manner in which the concept was implemented" (1983a). The United States, he contends, does not have any prisons resembling "what we return inmates to."

Summary Discussion of Programs

The programs described in this book are summarized in Table 1 (Page 46).

The table summarizes the programs at seventy-four state prisons in all fifty states and the District of Columbia, nine Federal institutions, and three Canadian institutions in three Canadian Provinces. The table is based on the programs and institutions described in chapter 8.

Chapter 7 contains a table providing a state-by-state breakdown of institutional programs for incarcerated mothers and children, as well as those in three Canadian institutions. Examination of the percentages permits us to compare the changes in programs between 1996 and 1985, when *Prisons and Kids* was first published. These comparisons should be made with caution, however. For example, the effort made in this work are more complete than in 1985; this results in California institutions being represented six times, and since the state permits conjugal visits, the percentage is slightly overrepresented; instead of 16.3 percent, the percentage would be slightly lower, if California and other states were counted only once. Nevertheless, the main trends are the following:

- Classes for inmates are still offered in almost all institutions, but the same caveat is necessary as in 1985. These classes vary among the institutions regarding their appropriateness for child development and parenting. In some cases, the institution may be reporting only the classes traditionally offered to all inmates, and not specifically those addressed to incarcerated mothers.
- "Family Visits" is a category that was introduced by some institutions to differentiate these from "Conjugal Visits." Although the two terms are often synonymous, "Family Visits" includes those institutions that may or may not also offer "Conjugal Visits."
- There has been a slight increase in the proportion of facilities allowing "Conjugal Visits." In addition to the six state institutions in California, conjugal visits are permitted in Connecticut, Maryland, Mississippi, New Jersey, New Mexico, New York, Washington, and the Canadian Prison for Women at Kingston, Ontario.
- The availability of "furloughs" for prisoners to visit with their families and children has declined. In this context, furloughs "after parole" or the traditional leaves for emergency purposes, funerals, or deathbed visits are not included in these totals and percentages.
- "Overnight visits" have declined slightly in the proportion of institutions making these visits available. However, some respondents distinguished between "overnight" and "extended" visits. Although six institutions did not offer "overnight" visits, "extended" visits were available or planned in Oregon, North Carolina, West Virginia, Idaho, and Newfoundland. In New Hamp-

Table 1
Summary of Programs for Incarcerated Mothers and Their Children in Fifty States, the District of Columbia, and Three Canadian Provinces
(Representing 86 Institutions and 40,758 Incarcerated Women)*

Programs	Present	Planned	Percent of All Institutions 1996	1985*
Classes for Inmates	82	1	96.5	98.0
Family Visits	62	0	72.1	—
Furloughs	43	0	50.0	90.2
Overnight Visits with Children	30	0	34.9	39.2
Children's Centers	25	3	32.6	45.1
Community Facilities for Mothers and their Children	23	1	27.9	9.8
Conjugal Visits	14	0	16.3	11.8
Prison Nurseries	4	1	5.8	2.0

*In 1985, fifty-one institutions were represented.

shire, extended visits are available to new mothers.

- There has been a decrease in the percentage of institutions with "Children's Centers" or "Day Care Centers." Hovever, centers are being planned in Indiana, Mississippi, and Pennsylvania.
- One of the most dramatic changes has been an increase in the proportion of jurisdictions that provide community facilities or residential facilities where sentenced mothers can live with their children while the mothers serve their sentences.
- There has been a slight increase in the proportion of facilities with "Prison Nurseries." Prison nurseries are present at the two New York women's institutions and in Nebraska, and in Manitoba.

Family Advocacy

As funds for programs for incarcerated parents have been reduced, volunteer organizations that support the families of inmates and assist in the maintenance of family ties while a parent is incarcerated have emerged. The programs described in this book are a specialized area or offshoot of what originated as the "family support movement" (Kagan and Weissbourd 1994b). The controversies and issues are essentially the same (Zigler 1994), but the focus is on a particularly high-risk group of families and children, incarcerated parents and their families. Therefore, the challenges are greater.

The strategies and solutions that have benefitted the family support movement should be applicable to the programs described here. However, in times of budget deficits, there is increased competition for limited funds. As programs increase and expand, Bruner (1994) mentions another type of competition—competition for services from existing community agencies.

The family resource and support programs were stimulated by the antipoverty programs of the Kennedy and Johnson administrations, which in the 1960s resulted in Head Start and Legal Aid, but their origins can be traced further back to the parent-education movement and the settlement house movement of the early twentieth century, as well as to self-help programs such as Alcoholics Anonymous (Weissbourd 1994).

The Fourth North American Conference on the Family and Corrections with the theme, "Exploring the Family Side of Justice," was held in Quebec, Canada, in 1993 (Proceedings 1993). Over 200 people from six countries attended.

In 1976, Sack *et al.* interviewed a small sample of incarcerated parents in Oregon and recommended a strategy of intervention that included family counseling and the inclusion of the family in any rehabilitation program for the prisoner. The rationale for such programs probably can be briefly summarized best by the following policy statement from the Second Chance program in Minnesota:

> Through these various components we are attempting to assist these women in preserving and restructuring the family unit during the incarceration while at the same time increasing their skills in parenting and helping them to plan for a smooth transition back to their parental caretaker role.

Bish *et al.* (1993) describe the "Pyramid Model" of a private, nonprofit organization, Families in Crisis, Inc., in Hartford, Connecticut. The model addresses a family's "hierarchy of needs" by providing interventions during certain crises of the family:

- *Stabilization Interventions:* "address acute emotional and economic needs that arise as a result of the offender's arrest, arraignment or sentencing (such as, outreach, crisis intervention, case management, counseling)."
- *Maintenance Interventions:* "empower families to maintain the stability and growth achieved by providing them with support for continued care and opportunities for meaningful interactions (such as, child care programs, support groups, transportation services)."
- *Enhancement Interventions:* "assist families to create meaningful change by providing programs that address dysfunction and teach new skills for healthy and productive living (such as parenting programs, anger management, postrelease reentry programs)."

Burton-Barnett and Cameron (1993) describe Project SEEK (Services to Enable and Empower Kids) and its evaluation. This project was started in Genesee County, Michigan (the largest city in the county is Flint) in December 1988. It is a collaborative effort involving the Michigan Departments of Mental Health, Social Services, and Corrections; the Mott Children's Health Center; and Genesee County Community Mental Health.

> The project is designed to break the cycle of intergenerational criminality by providing support and reducing stress for families and children, improving discipline and limit-setting, increasing pro-social behavior and improving school performance.

The project provides services to the families and children of fathers who are incarcerated for less than seven years. The home-based outreach services that are provided to these families and children are the following: case management, support groups for the children, support groups for caregivers, tutoring, training in problem-solving techniques, facilitating communication with the inmate parent, advocating for the children and caregivers with other service systems, and parenting training for the inmates.

Some evaluation results for Project SEEK (as of June 1992) include the following:

- The service group caregivers rate their

children higher in cognitive skills than the control group caregivers.

- Service group children score higher on academic self-esteem than the control group children at twelve months.
- "The mean number of times service group children changed schools was significantly fewer than control group children one year after intake."
- "Within a relatively short time, concerns about basic needs and social support decrease dramatically."
- "Concerns about chemical dependency, parenting, and caregiver's psychological well-being do not diminish substantially until a family has participated in the program for over two years."

Selber *et al.* (1993) describe the Family Support Program in Texas that was initiated in 1991. This is a collaborative effort between the School of Social Work at the University of Texas-Austin and the Texas Department of Criminal Justice's Institutional Division and the Pardons and Paroles Division, with funding from the Texas Governor's Office of Criminal Justice. The program developed a plan to identify and activate "natural support networks" for ex-offenders being released from Texas prisons to reduce recidivism.

Several weeks before the release of a family member from prison, the family receives "assistance in locating financial services, social services, counseling, employment services and supportive associations" to assist the family "in coping with the needs of the ex-offender and improving the ability of the family to locate and utilize community social agencies and employment opportunities." Family Support Program is targeted for inmates released to Travis County who will live with a family member. An evaluation comparing the Family Support Program service population with a "matched or control group" shows that "80 percent of the Family Support Program participants are identified as on a 'Normal Reporting' status compared to 66 percent of the control group." The reduced recidivism rate of the Family Support Program clients represents a savings of $1,647,984, based on an average cost of $45.70 a day if these persons had been incarcerated.

Genesis II for Women, Inc., in Minnesota, offers The Criminal Justice Project, established in 1976, which serves as an alternative to incarceration for women who are referred through municipal or district court. The Maternal Guidance Project of this group, was established in 1981 and seeks to improve the parenting and independent living skills of mothers who have been referred from child protection for the abuse and/or neglect of their children. These programs offer individualized counseling and group therapy, an Indian Women's Support Group, independent living skill classes, adult basic education/GED preparation, career development classes with the assistance of the Minneapolis Technical Institute, parenting education, and daycare.

Aid to Inmate Mothers (AIM), Inc. is a non-profit, volunteer program founded in 1987 as a committee of the Alabama Prison Projects. Its purpose is to help incarcerated mothers at the Julia Tutwiler Prison maintain positive relationships with their children. Every month volunteers from around the state bring children to visit their mothers for a day-long visit. "AIM operates the Community Outreach Program which provides family support during and after time in prison and helps meet special needs." An inmate board enables the mothers to have a voice in prison affairs relating to the AIM visits, and "a mother's forum meets once a month to discuss ideas and problems that arise from the visits." Volunteers from a branch of AIM also provide child custody education and transportation at the Massachusetts Correctional Institution at Framingham.

The Edwin Gould Services for Children agency in New York City initiated an "Incarcerated Mothers Program" in 1986. The program's caseworkers help "incarcerated mothers, children, and their families to prevent children from being placed into foster care and to strengthen families' capacities to maintain themselves as functioning units" (Immarigeon 1994).

Another program with similar goals is Hooper House in New York City. It was established by the Women's Prison Association and works with the New York City Child Welfare Administration (Immarigeon, 1994). It is a residential facility designed to "integrate foster care prevention services with alternatives to incarceration . . . The foster care prevention services are intended to either keep the children of female offenders out of foster care or to reduce children's length of stay in foster care."

The "Kids Need Moms, Inc." program was started in June 1991, when it was completely funded by the women at the Florence Crane Women's Facility in Coldwater, Michigan. Subsequently, it became a nonprofit organization that relies on volunteers. It has obtained funding from the Kellogg Foundation and the Michigan Department of Social Services. It offers child development classes, family counseling, legal assistance, and transportation for children.

Project REACH at the Metro Correctional Institution in Atlanta, Georgia serves as a liaison for inmates and their families with community organizations, such as, the "Mothers in Prison" project, Aid to Imprisoned Mothers, Inc. (AIM), Karen Nelson Ministries, Prison Ministries With Women, and the Tender Mercies Ministries. These organizations provide transportation, legal services, and other assistance. The Georgia Correctional Dental Society also is active in providing services to the women and children.

The use of volunteers in providing supportive service has been described by Fishman and Alissi (1979). The special pilot project, "Women in Crisis," in Hartford, Connecticut, relied on volunteers in an advocacy role for the inmates and their families. Their primary goal is to strengthen the relationship between inmates and their families. They assist a family in their initial visit to a loved one in prison and provide the family with support during the initial six- to eight-week adjustment period of the inmate's incarceration.

The Prison Fellowship ministry, founded by Charles Colson, started its "Angel Tree" program in Alabama in the late 1970s (Simbro 1995). The program, working with prison officials, collects from prisoners the names and addresses of their children. These names are given "to participating churches, and volunteers call the inmate's families to ask for the children's gift wishes—usually toys and clothes. In December, volunteers set up a Christmas tree in the participating church. It is decorated with paper angels; on each is written the gift request of a prisoner's child. Church members then choose angels and buy presents—what the child asked for, if possible. Near Christmas, volunteers deliver the gifts to the child's home or distribute them at church-sponsored parties."

In addition, at the Iowa Correctional Institution for Women at Mitchellville, Prison Fellowship provides seminars, bible studies, and transportation to allow children to visit their incarcerated parent, and support groups. The Salvation Army program "Toy List" has goals similar to the "Angel Tree" program.

The Family & Corrections Network is a not-for-profit organization, formed in 1983, whose long-term goal is "for family programs and services to become a standard component of all stages of the criminal justice process." The Network provides information and support "to those providing services to families of prisoners in the United States and Canada." Jim Mustin, its executive director, cites some of the research that shows that the maintenance of strong family ties while in prison has a positive relationship with parole success (*Family & Corrections Network Reports* 1994, 1995).

Mustin (1991) proposes a "reordering of priorities for corrections" so that contacts between the offender and his or her family can be maximized. Some of the services he proposes are training of correctional caseworkers to increase their work with the family; providing information to families on the criminal justice system and on sources of assistance; giving emotional support and counseling; locating temporary shelter and transportation; and mediation of disputes between the families and prison management. In addition, Mustin suggests:

> . . .(T)he families of offenders can potentially fill a great gap in the correctional system—the lack of a political constituency. Corrections needs an informed group of citizens who care about the day-to-day conditions of both staff and offenders and who will take these concerns to elected officials. Families of offenders can become that constituency. This process has already begun in Texas and California where political interest groups of families and friends of offenders have influenced legislative and executive processes impacting corrections.

Adalist-Estrin (1994) focuses on the "collaboration between family support and criminal justice" that is needed to achieve the following goal: "reordering of social priorities that goes beyond the rhetoric of maintaining family ties and includes collective commitment to supporting the growth and development of relationships within inmates' families." More recently Adalist-Estrin (1995) describes programs that "hold families together in an effort to decrease recidivism and combat the ever-increasing intergenerational patterns of criminality." She emphasizes the need for further research and evaluation of such programs.

Meltzler (1994) describes several family advocacy programs, including the benefits from prison nurseries and community correctional programs. Benefits include: reduced costs, and lower recidivism that accompany the maintenance of strong family ties. The author concludes, "If the children can be saved from the criminal justice and welfare systems, the potential savings are incalculable."

The Las Comadres Program in California "locates volunteer foster mothers mostly for newborn babies of incarcerated mothers. Las Comadres coordinates an informal arrangement between the mother and the foster parent in which the foster parent raises the child during the mother's prison term and ensures family unity through frequent visitations" (Blakeley, letter of January 4, 1996).

Poe (1995) describes a new approach provided for grandparents who become caregivers for their grandchildren when the parent is incarcerated. The approach is "Grandparents As Parents" (GAP). Although the approach was started by Syl de Toledo in Long Beach, California, a number of similar programs exist throughout the United States. GAP programs offer support groups for grandparents in which the caregivers can share their problems and solutions, listen to presentations from experts in various relevant fields, obtain information about referrals to community agencies, receive respite care, and obtain actual resources, such as clothing and emergency groceries.

Other authors describe programs and practices useful to those examining programs for incarcerated parents. Bloom (1995) presents a number of child protective services practices that would benefit parents and their children at the time of arrest, and during incarceration to assist in reunification, and in improving correctional policies and practices. Marcus (1995) recommends greater collaboration between child welfare and correctional systems so that services for incarcerated parents and their children are more "family-friendly."

A number of community organizations actively urge the decarceration of inmate mothers and support alternatives to prison. In Iowa, the Friends of Prisoners at Mitchelville (the women's prison) was formed "following the dissolution by the present warden of the public advisory board for the prison" (memo from Rev. Carlos Jayne, May 1996). Its mission, adopted in February 1993, is as follows:

- Advocate for humanitarian administration
- Advocate for increased use of volunteers
- Advocate for a statewide humanitarian attitude to support the goal of rehabilitation
- Advocate for alternatives to imprisonment for those who can be rehabilitated more effectively in another environment
- Advocate for responding to the special needs of women.

Another group, The Justice Works Community in Brooklyn, New York, is a grassroots program founded in 1992 with the long-term goal to change sentencing policy and to "establish alternatives to incarceration as the sentencing norm for mothers with dependent children."

On May 11, 1996, the day before Mother's Day, it organized an annual rally in several cities to support its program: Mothers in Prison, Children in Crises. Rallies were held in Atlanta, Boston, Boulder, Des Moines, Detroit, Indianapolis, Little Rock, Nashville, New York, Pittsburgh, San Antonio, and St. Louis to call attention to the plight of women in prison. This nonprofit organization serves as a network of 350 secular and religious organizations in bringing "the mainstream community into direct dialogue with female ex-prisoners and their families and organizing for change."

Breen (1995a) describes successful advocacy efforts in California and concludes, "Advocacy by its very nature is not a one-time type of activity. Change comes very slowly, especially when it concerns a population of children living in the dark shadow of the wave of 'Get Tough on Crime' legislation sweeping across the country today."

3. Legal Issues

The literature on legal issues surrounding incarcerated mothers and pregnant inmates stresses the deprivation of prisoners' rights and offers strategies for correcting unconstitutional conditions (Barry et al. 1995, Brodie 1982, Holt 1981-82, McHugh 1980). Unfortunately, standards promulgated by various professional groups generally have not been supported by research. Holt (1981-82) concludes additional standards are not the answer and litigation by inmates is the best way to achieve reforms. "The desire to achieve penological goals must be balanced against the need to preserve ordinary human rights."

Legal actions can be brought by individual prisoners or through class action suits based upon the Eighth Amendment (cruel and unusual punishment), the Fourteenth Amendment (due process and equal protection), and tort claims if the state fails to provide adequate care and protection, or on custody cases based on the *best interest of the child* yardstick (Holt 1981-82).

Class Action Suits

Daly *et al.* (1988) describe a class action suit by the inmates at the Connecticut Correctional Institution for Women at Niantic (*West v. Manson*, Civ. No. H83-366, D. Conn. 1983). The complaints were based on a violation of due process; inmates' right to be free of cruel and unusual punishment; a violation of the plaintiffs' rights to family integrity, as guaranteed by the First, Ninth, and Fourteenth Amendments; a violation of the inmates' constitutional right of access to the courts; and a violation of the equal protection clause of the Fourteenth Amendment by intentionally failing to provide facilities, programs, and care for the women inmates that was comparable to those provided to male inmates. Daly details the use of social scientific research in the interviewing of 126 women prisoners that resulted in a settlement with the state of Connecticut, one week prior to the trial date.

As a consequence of this, the Niantic women gained a new sense of power. As of November 1987, the authors state that they were renegotiating issues raised in the original complaint, as well as two more issues: AIDS, and gross crowding. Glasser's evaluation of the Niantic Parenting Program (1990) states that as the settlement was taking place in 1983, a "Creative Arts" program was being implemented. A Parenting Program (described previously) was federally funded from July 1987 through September 1990.

Deck (1988), citing *Bailey v. Lombard* (101 Misc. 2d, 420 N.Y.S. 2d, 1979) states that several factors were set forth to consider in analyzing whether separation is in a child's best interests:

- "Availability of facilities adequate to insure the child's health and safety"
- "The mother's psychological health and parenting background"
- "The crime for which the mother was convicted as it might reflect upon her parenting capabilities"
- "The length of the mother's sentence"

Kimbrell (1994) describes one of the efforts of the Georgia Legal Services Program that resulted in the closing of the Women's Correctional Institution at Hardwick in September 1993. In the mid-1980s, Georgia Legal Services Program filed suit charging unconstitutional conditions at the institution (*Cason v. Seckinger*, M.D. Ga, 1984). In the spring of 1993, one of the original plaintiffs contacted Georgia Legal Services Program about a medical complaint. She said she was forced to abort a pregnancy that resulted from intercourse with a prison guard. "Eventually, more than 190 women came forth to claim they had had sexual contact with prison staff." The plaintiffs sought an order of contempt related to the Cason case. " Several prison guards and staff were criminally charged as a result of the inmates' charges."

A class action suit brought by women inmates at the Iowa Correctional Institution for Women at Mitchellville (*Pargo et al. v. Elliott et al.*, U.S. Dist. Court, S.D., Iowa) questioned whether the state of Iowa provides women inmates equal protection under the Fourteenth Amendment. The women inmates believe there is sexual discrimination in educational, vocational, and recreational programs; job training opportunities; counseling; rehabilitative opportunities; prerelease opportunities (including furloughs), and other policies and procedures. The trial court found that applying the Klinger court's equal protection analysis (*Klinger v. Nebraska Dept. of Corrections* (31 F. 3d 727, 8th Cir. 1994), in the Iowa Correctional Institution for Women, female inmates are not similarly situated to male inmates in Iowa due to its small population and the segregation of female inmates from male inmates.

On appeal, after comparing the women's institution with the men's institutions in Iowa on total population, age, education, sentences, security levels, offenses, number of sentences per inmates, and custody, the court found and the Eighth Circuit Court of Appeals agreed (November 13, 1995) that the women and men inmates in Iowa are "not similarly situated," that the differences are based on legitimate concerns for security and rehabilitation, and that these were not "gender-motivated." The trial court judge stated, "The Fourteenth Amendment guarantees equal laws, not equal results" (citing *Feeney*, 442 U.S. at 273). The comparisons of *institutions* may be flawed, however, and more appropriate comparisons would have been of similar categories of women and men incarcerated in Iowa's prisons.

Barry *et al.* (1995) cite cases in support of visitation rights for prisoners, as well as the First Circuit Court of Appeals in *Feeley v. Sampson* (1978) stating that visitation rights, besides having to meet the . . . due process standard, reflect First Amendment values, most clearly the rights of association.

Ashman (1982) summarizes the decision of the Supreme Court of California in a case dealing with overnight visitation (*In re Cummings*, February 18, 1982, 180 Cal. Rptr. 826). The court concluded that "in the absence of a valid, provable family relationship based on blood, marriage, or adoption, prison officials are justified in denying extended overnight visitation." The court upheld "an administrative regulation excluding family visitation by persons having only a 'common-law relationship' . . . " The court stated that the program's "social purpose of preserving family unity would not be served by encouraging an inmate's overnight visits with those who are not in his family."

An Iowa Supreme Court decision in 1973 (*Bowen v. Bowen*) replaced the "tender years' doctrine" or ("maternal presumption") with the "best interests of the child" standard in this custody case. Although the bonding issue was not crucial to this case, the decision coincides with a trend away from the earlier emphasis placed on mother-child bonding.

An Iowa custody case found the state statute terminating parental rights due to incarceration of a parent to be "unconstitutionally vague." The statute did not specifically mention incarcerated parents but provided for termination for the following reasons:

> That the parents are unfit by reasons of debauchery, intoxication, habitual use of narcotic drugs, repeated lewd and lascivious behavior, or other conduct found by the court likely to be detrimental to the physical or mental health or morals of the child (Code of Iowa, 232.41(2)(a), 1975).

In *Alsager v. District Court of Polk County, Iowa* (406 F. Supp. 10, S.D. Iowa, 1975), "the court considered the state's interest in protecting children yet found in favor of a parent's interest in raising children in an environment free from governmental interference" (Haley 1977, p. 150). It is not clear whether this ruling can be resolved to accommodate a mother's desire to raise her child within a governmental institution. Reflecting adherence to the concept of *maternal presumption*, Haley stresses the importance of the first three years of a child's development. "During the tender years the mother is the focal point of the child's existence. When the mother is imprisoned, she is unable to play the pivotal role in her child's maturation that would otherwise be hers."

The literature on the legal issues contains recommended reforms, which include prison nurseries (*Yale Law Journal* 1978), "mother-release" programs similar to work release (Palmer 1972), community residences for women offenders and their children since the "prison is no place to carry or give birth to a baby" (McHugh 1980, p. 259), and suggestions for legislative reform (Palmer 1972).

Metzler (1994) describes "pending" federal legislation (HR569, introduced January 25, 1993, and SB 1158, introduced June 24, 1993) that "would provide funds to establish one federal and four state community correctional facilities to house eligible prisoners and their children." If passed by Congress, the "Family Unity Demonstration Project Act" would "allow children less than six years of age to live with their mothers in a residential facility" and receive parenting education, substance abuse treatment, and job training. However, Metzler adds that similar legislation was passed by the Illinois legislature in 1991, but, "To date, no such program has been initiated in the state."

Best Interests of the Child

Brodie (1982) has addressed constitutional issues and reviewed state statutes on custody determination. She writes, "By implication, considerations of the availability of facilities within prisons, the extra planning required, and the effect of the arrangement on the rest of the prison population should be secondary to the needs of the child." She presents the following criteria used by courts in custody cases for determining the best interests of a child.

1. It is to the child's benefit to remain with its natural parent.
2. The child's needs are best served by continuity of care from a specific individual. This has implications for the incarcerated mother's plans to resume care of her child upon release.
3. The caregiver must be physically and emotionally capable of raising her child. This could be determined by an examination of the incarcerated mother by medical doctors and psychologists.
4. The moral character of the mother should be considered, but incarceration should not be assumed as evidence of unfitness.
5. The department would be expected to provide the "nominal expenditures" necessary for the material needs of the child.
6. A consideration of the child's age, or the "tender years' doctrine," was first enunciated in Virginia in *Mullen v. Mullen* (1948). It illustrates the principle that as long as the mother is fit, there is a rebuttable inference that a child's place is with the mother, particularly in those cases where the child is of tender years. The Superior Court of Virginia does not apply this to the rights of parents, but to the right of the child. "The presumption is, in fact, an inference society has drawn that such right is best served when a child of tender years is awarded the

custodial care of its mother," according to *McCreery v. McCreery* (1977).

Brodie adds, "Just as the child's best interest must be considered in custody disputes between natural parents, it is clear the reasoning of the tender years doctrine is equally applicable where the mother is incarcerated." She concludes:

> The question of whether a woman who gives birth while incarcerated should be allowed to keep her child with her is in a state of flux. In the final analysis, the solution must balance the needs of the prison officials, the state, and the incarcerated woman with paramount attention given to the needs of the individual child. While opponents point to the dangers of prison life, it is essential to recognize that their catastrophic predictions have not materialized in those states which have experimented with the idea. For instance, no child has been held hostage. Children face comparable dangers in the free world. All of their dangers are speculative and one does the best one can to protect children from them. The potential physical risk does not outweigh the recognized emotional benefits the child receives from being with its mother. The best way to ensure in the balancing process that the child's best interests are the pivotal factor, is to decide on a case-by-case basis, as called for in *Wainwright v. Moore*, (374 So. 2nd 5486, Florida District Court of Appeals, 1979) whether an individual child should be cared for by its inmate mother.

Sametz (1980) contrasted the "best interests" standard with the "least detrimental interest" standard, saying the issue is a matter of the child's physical well-being or overall welfare versus the child's instinctive and emotional needs. "In using the least detrimental interests standard, the court recognizes its limited ability to predict the child's future relationship with an adult who is not the child's biological parent." The child is seen as a victim of circumstance, which promotes a speedy custody decision. "By avoiding the use of the best interests' standard, the court does not weigh the child's rights against the adult's rights, but views the rights of all parties on an equal basis" (Sametz 1980).

Permanency Planning

Genty (1995) cites "at least twenty-five states" that "have termination-of-parental rights or adoption statutes that explicitly per-

tain to incarcerated parents." He writes:

> Disruption of families through incarceration of the parents has become an increasingly serious problem over the past decade. In addition to growing numbers of parents who are separated from their children by incarceration, increasing sentence lengths mean that these families are being kept apart for longer periods of time.

Genty suggests a number of "affirmative efforts" that can be made by the state to support and strengthen the family. His suggestions are similar to those of other authors.

Public Law 96-272, the Adoption Assistance and Child Welfare Reform Act of 1980 describes Barry *et al.* (1995) as seeking "to support eventual reunification" of the incarcerated parent and children. Beckerman (1994) suggests the following "prerequisite conditions" for the mother's involvement in permanency planning:

1. There need to be correspondence and telephone contacts between the mother and the caseworker. A high rate of illiteracy sometimes limits correspondence, and prison and agency policies may restrict telephone contacts.
2. The prerequisite conditions for imprisoned mothers to attend court hearings are that they receive timely notification and are provided transportation. Only 68 percent of the mothers studied by Beckerman received notification of upcoming court hearings.
3. Prison caseworkers could "work collaboratively with officials in correctional facilities to establish clear procedures for notifying mothers of upcoming hearings, familiarizing them with the procedures to obtain transportation to hearings, and ensuring that such procedures are followed."

Barry *et al.* (1995) cite a number of reasons why the services available are "often insufficient" to take advantage of this legislation:

1. Notifications of court proceedings are "often insufficient" and not timely.
2. Incarcerated parents are unable to obtain permission and arrange transportation to be present in court.
3. Social service and judicial agencies do not clearly state the necessary dates, addresses, and procedures.
4. Beckerman (1994) adds: state agencies may not work with incarcerated parents to prepare the necessary individual case plans.
5. It is difficult for incarcerated parents to take advantage of this and other statutes without legal representation. Barry *et al.* point out that " . . . incarcerated parents only have a right to a court-appointed attorney if their parental rights are in danger of being terminated" and not in matters regarding visitation. In the latter case, the prisoners must either represent themselves or find an attorney who will assist them "pro bono" (Barry *et al.* 1995).

One of the accomplishments of The Georgia Legal Services Program has been a class action suit filed in 1980 to enforce the Adoption Assistance and Child Welfare Act (*J. J. v. Ledbetter*, S.D. Ga. 1985). The district court "eventually determined that parents were entitled to a fair hearing at the reduction, denial, or termination of services for children in foster care. The court found that the county Department of Family and Children Services offices were required to allow parents access to their protective-services files and provide reunification services. When the Georgia Legal Services Program requested the department to bring a client's two children to visit her at the women's prison, they refused, but an administrative hearing resulted in the mother receiving a reunification case plan and visitation with her children. Subsequently, the state adopted regulations providing that "parents in prison are entitled to a case plan and visitation services that allow them to keep in contact with their children" (Kimbrell 1994).

Smith (1995) presents the following recommendations that would assist incarcerated parents in avoiding the termination of their parental rights:

1. State legislatures should consider a wider range of sentencing alternatives to imprisonment for primary caregiver parents.
2. States should allocate funds for parent-child visitations.
3. Closer attention should be paid to the screening, training, and support of caregivers.
4. Prison crowding may reduce the opportunities for incarcerated parents to obtain services for the problems that led to their incarceration. Correctional institutions should provide parenting classes, individual and joint parent-child counseling, substance abuse treatment, counseling for survivors of childhood sexual abuse and domestic violence, and vocational/educational programs to help parents become employable.
5. Legal counseling and representation should be available to incarcerated parents.
6. "Open adoptions" should be supported. "The concept of permanency planning for children was implemented in the 1980s to prevent foster care drift and to assure permanent homes for children whose parents could not care for them. However, in our willingness to address the failures of the foster care system, we have failed to take into account children's needs to maintain a bond with their parents. The widespread passage of statutes to permit parents and adopted children ongoing contact would make it easier for parents with very long sentences to obtain permanency for their children without having to sever their relationship."

Norman (1995) also discusses the issues related to foster care and permanency planning for incarcerated parents and their children. The author concludes:

> While there are fundamental similarities in the experience of foster care for all children, children of prisoners and their parents have significantly different experiences in the areas of visitation, family reunification services, and the outcomes of placement. These differences may lead to a different rate of termination of parental rights among incarcerated parents, and should be explored with further research.

At the Massachusetts Correctional Institution at Framingham, coordinated efforts with the Department of Social Services resulted in on-site Foster Care Reviews and supervised visits for inmates whose children are in the custody of the department.

Chesney-Lind and Immarigeon (1995) have recommended a "moratorium on the construction of women's prisons" and emphasize the "decarceration" of women offenders. They describe programs in several states that rely on alternatives to imprisonment, such as the following:

- specialized bail units
- reclassification of such offenses as prostitution and the possession of small amounts of marijuana
- supervised home release
- day care provisions
- an increase in pretrial supervised release
- more residential substance abuse treatment programs
- specialized probation and parole caseloads for women

- contracts with private agencies to provide services and referrals to agencies in the community. The authors caution, however, that these community-based alternatives would need to be "complemented by the creation of a political and social climate receptive to the decarceration of women."

In another publication, Immarigeon (1994) also emphasizes the need for alternatives to incarceration. He summarizes the New York legislation (Chapter 911 of the laws of 1983) in which incarcerated parents are entitled to the delivery of social services at the prison, prison system cooperation with the child welfare system, and even the right to visit their children outside of the prison if appropriate. With this law, the legislature eliminated the automatic loss of parental rights upon a mother's or father's incarceration.

However, *In Matter of Kareem B.*, 1989 WL 73108, (*National Law Journal* 1989) "evidence establishing permanent neglect was sufficient to justify the termination of parental rights of two incarcerated fathers," the New York Court of Appeals ruled on July 6, 1989, affirming three lower court decisions. The case involved two fathers who would be incarcerated beyond their children's age of minority. "Though the fathers had attempted to place the children with relatives for the duration of their imprisonment, they were unable to do so, and thus placed the children in foster care." The 1983 statute was intended to prevent the fathers from losing their parental rights because of their incarceration.

> While incarcerated, however, the parent must fulfill the obligations of a parent to the extent that he or she cooperate with the authorized child-care agency in planning for the child's future and in arranging visits with the child. The amended statutory scheme is designed to take into account the special circumstances of an incarcerated parent. Nevertheless, if the parent, with the help of the agency, cannot either plan for the child's future or maintain contact with the child, that parent, the Court of Appeals determined, may have permanently neglected the child, thus justifying termination of his or her parental rights. The threshold determination in a neglect proceeding is whether the child-care agency exercised diligent efforts to strengthen and nurture the parent-child relationship. Having determined that the agencies exercised due diligence, the Court of Appeals in this case next examined the individual efforts of the parent to maintain contact with, as well as to plan for the future of his child. The plan for the future of the child must be both "reasonable and feasible." Each respondent offered a plan to keep his child in foster care, while maintaining contact, until his release. The appellate division in each case rejected such a plan stating that it was neither a viable nor realistic option. The Court of Appeals affirmed.

The recent California legislation, "Pregnant and Parenting Women's Alternative Sentencing Program Act," has been described earlier (Blakeley 1995).

After suggesting seven affirmative efforts, Genty concludes (1995):

> However, even if the guidelines suggested above are followed, the problems associated with parental incarceration will remain; indeed, those problems can probably only be solved by implementing alternatives to incarceration so that parents who are their children's primary caretakers are no longer being imprisoned. Sadly, such a radical rethinking of our criminal justice system is not likely to occur in the near future.

Medical Care

As a result of the increase in the incarceration rate over the past decade, particularly for women, there has been an increase in class action suits that focus on the adequacy of medical care for pregnant prisoners. Five such suits described by Barry *et al.* (1995) were filed in California between 1985 and 1989.

> Prosecutions have occurred in more than 20 states and the District of Columbia in the last 10 years, and certain states such as South Carolina have been particularly punitive toward pregnant, substance-dependent women. In some instances, the "charges" lodged against pregnant women are less criminal in nature than moralistic.

> (The authors acknowledge that)
> while some judges who incarcerate pregnant substance-dependent women appear to do so simply to punish these women, many judges are genuinely concerned about ensuring that pregnant substance-dependent women receive adequate prenatal care and do not continue to use drugs or alcohol during their pregnancies.

Wooldredge and Masters (1993) found (in their survey of wardens cited previously) that although all facilities provide medical resources and services for the inmates in general, only twenty-nine facilities (or 48 percent of their sample of sixty-one institutions) have "written policies related specifically to the medical care of pregnant inmates." These services include the following:

- prenatal care (n = 29, or 48 percent)
- networks with community agencies which provide "other" prenatal care (n = 23, or 38 percent)
- Lamaze classes (n = 10, or 16 percent)
- special diets and nutritional allowances (n = 9, or 15 percent).
- abortions and abortion counseling (n = 5, or 9 percent)
- full-time nurse or midwife available—just for pregnant inmates (n = 5, or 9 percent)

The Massachusetts Correctional Institution at Framingham operates the "Catch the Hope" Perinatal Clinic which provides medical and social services to pregnant and postpartum inmates. The staff consists of the Perinatal Nurse Coordinator and the Perinatal Case Manager. The programs include:

- pregnancy screening according to protocols established by the medical care provider
- coordination of medical services offered to pregnant and postpartum women
- counseling, education, and case management that includes a weekly prenatal group; individual counseling, as well as treatment and discharge planning, including a review of options for transfer or parole and referral to the Neil J. Houston House; the labor support program which identifies professional labor attendants who volunteer to accompany pregnant inmates through labor and delivery in the hospital; an audio education program which offers birth- and parenting-related audio cassettes to qualified inmates; and referral to treatment upon release.

Another medical issue for women is AIDS. Bates (1989) summarizes some of the court cases that deal with conjugal visiting, the AIDS crisis, and the medical needs of inmates.

In 1994, AIDS was the leading cause of death among all Americans twenty-five to forty-four years old, outstripping homicide, suicide, heart disease, and cancer. At year end 1994, 2.3 percent of the 999,693 State and Federal prison inmates in the United States were infected with the human immunodeficiency virus (HIV) (Bureau of Justice Statistics 1996, 1995b). In state prisons, 2.5 percent (21,749 inmates) were HIV positive; in Federal prisons, 1.1 percent (964 inmates) were HIV positive. Of all inmates in United States' prisons, 4,849 (0.5 percent) had confirmed AIDS. In 1994, 955 state inmates died of AIDS-related causes compared to 520 in 1991. In 1994 AIDS-related causes accounted for over half of all inmate deaths in New York (60 percent); Connecticut (60 percent); Florida (56 percent), Massachusetts (54 percent); and New Jersey (51 percent). Since November 1985, it is estimated that more than 4,500 inmates have died of AIDS (National Institute of Justice 1995).

At the end of 1994, there were 19,762 male inmates who tested HIV-positive (2.4 percent of the total custody population) compared to 1,953 female inmates (3.9 percent of the population). "Since 1991 the number of male state inmates infected with HIV has increased 22 percent, while the number of female inmates infected has increased at a much faster rate—69 percent" (Bureau of Justice Statistics 1996).

A survey conducted by Abt Associates, Inc. between May and December, 1994 (National Institute of Justice 1995) found "a number of interesting discrepancies" between state correctional systems' central office policies regarding HIV/AIDS and selected individual facilities' policies. This survey found AIDS incidence rates of 518 per 100,000 inmates in state/Federal institutions; 706 per 100,000 in city/county jails (in 1994-1995); compared to 41 per 100,000 in the total United States population in 1993. "Aggregate AIDS incidence rates in state/Federal systems were 464 cases per 100,000 among men and 705 cases among women." The report describes some of the inmate peer programs that deal with HIV/AIDS, including the "well-known and exemplary" ACE program at the Bedford Hills women's facility, and its community-based component (ACE-OUT) for former inmates with HIV.

Other programs described are Project O.A.S.I.S. (Oregon AIDS Support [Inmate] Services) at Oregon State Penitentiary (founded by an inmate in 1994); the program at the California Medical Facility at Vacaville; and the one at Louisiana State Penitentiary at Angola (established in October, 1993). Five state prison systems allow conjugal visits to HIV-infected prisoners; in California, HIV-infected inmates are excluded from conjugal visits. Some of the legal issues that have been raised by inmates are presented in this report and include the protection from harm by fellow inmates; challenges to mandatory testing and other testing policies; confidentiality; segregation and housing assignments; access to programs; and the adequacy of medical care. The Abt Associates report discusses preventive measures (such as the distribution of condoms and sterile syringes).

The National Commission on Correctional Health Care, a nonprofit organization, issued a position statement on HIV in corrections (National Commission 1994) that addresses HIV testing, segregation, education and counseling, prevention, confidentiality, consideration for parole and medical furloughs, correctional workers, and tuberculosis testing.

The National Commission's position is the following:

> . . .While the Commission clearly does not condone illegal activity by inmates, the terminal absoluteness of this disease, coupled with the potential for catastrophic epidemic, require (consistent with security) the unorthodox conduct of making available to inmates whatever appropriate protective devices can reduce the risk of contagion.

A 1994 study by the California Department of Health Services' Office of AIDS, in cooperation with the California Department of Corrections, "tested 5,000 inmates entering six CDC reception centers" (*CorrectCare*, 1995). The study "found 2.4 percent of male inmates and 3.2 percent of female inmates were infected with the HIV virus. This is relatively unchanged from the 1988 test results of 2.5 percent for male inmates and 3.1 percent for female inmates. The HIV seroprevalence rate for the community at large is reported to be 0.4 percent." The study also found hepatitis B virus among 47.9 percent of the female inmates and 32.1 percent of the male inmates; and hepatitis C viruses among 54.5 percent of the women and 39.4 percent of the men. Since the same risk factors are associated with HIV and hepatitis (injection drug use, tattooing, and unsafe sex), the report warns "of a potential for significant future growth in HIV/AIDS throughout California and the nation."

A court case challenging the Alabama Department of Corrections' policy of testing all inmates for HIV and segregating those who tested positive was upheld by the eleventh Circuit United States Court of Appeals (Criminal Justice Newsletter, October 1, 1991). The court "acknowledged that most states have decided against blanket segregation of HIV-positive inmates, but said it could not find that the policy was so far removed from legitimate correctional goals as to render it a Constitutional violation of the inmates' rights." Alabama has "placed all HIV-positive inmates, including those who have not shown any signs of illness, in special units at the Limestone Correctional Center at Capshaw and the Julia Tutwiler Prison for Women at Wetumpka. Approximately 180 inmates are currently held in those units."

Liability

The issue of liability was discussed by the legal counsel of the Wisconsin Department of Health and Social Services in giving tentative approval for day-long visits of children with their mothers at the Taycheedah Correctional Institution (correspondence of March 18, 1983):

1. The department does not feel that a state institution needs to be licensed as a child care giving institution to provide for extended visitations.
2. Regarding medical care, guardians should sign consent forms in advance to ensure emergency medical treatment. In life-threatening situations, the institution is responsible for providing an ambulance and first aid. The institution has considerable flexibility as to whether to provide medical treatment on the institution's grounds.
3. Transportation to and from the institution depends on its availability and who is to provide it. If provided by the state, the state is liable only if found negligent.
4. The institution's liability to the child or to the child's property while at the institution is the same as to any other visitor. The institution is responsible for using "ordinary care" to protect children from harm caused by an inmate, another child, or a staff member.
5. The institution must use ordinary care to prevent injury to the child by its mother. It must use care in screening for eligibility to participate in the program. This includes determining whether there is evidence of past sexual abuse or injury by the mother or another person.

4. Administration

Private Sector Corrections

With the increase in prison populations in the past ten years, and the corresponding prison construction accompanied by budgetary constraints, there has been greater interest in the privatization of corrections. The Wackenhut Corrections Corporation of Coral Gables, Florida, and the Corrections Corporation of America (CCA) in Nashville, Tennessee are just two of the corporations that are involved in the construction and management of entire facilities. Other corporations provide food services, medical services, and other services to existing or planned correctional facilities.

The Corrections Corporation of America was founded in 1983. From that date, private sector corrections has grown to more than 50,000 beds in 1995, for which Corrections Corporation of America has contracted for about half of these. Corrections Corporation of America opened the first privately built and operated women's prison in the United States in June 1989. The New Mexico Women's Correctional Facility in Grants, New Mexico was originally built for 204 beds, but it was expanded to 322 beds in 1995. In Australia, the Corrections Corporation of America will be building and managing a 125-bed women's prison in Victoria. It will be the first women's prison in Australia, and it is scheduled to open in June 1996.

In Texas alone, there are five prisons run by either Wackenhut or Corrections Corporation of America. The women's prison at Lockhart is operated by Wackenhut. According to Ernest Gremillion, Assistant Warden, "We are currently conducting program needs assessments to determine the focus of programming for 1996. Once defined, programs will be developed and delivered" (letter of December 20, 1995).

In Des Moines, Iowa, the Women's Correctional Facility was built by and is under the administration of the Fifth Judicial District, but is managed by the DTH Corporation of Dunn, North Carolina, with a subcontract for the treatment component with Right Turn, Inc. of Lynn, Massachusetts.

At Draper, Utah, the Pre-Release Facility for women at the Utah State Prison is operated under a private contract with the Management Training Corporation of Ogden, Utah.

Planning and Program Development

To be effective, family programs must be planned and become part of the budget. Couturier offers some suggestions on how to establish family programs (1995):

- Provide correctional administrators with information showing that these programs "represent good management tools that help foster a more positive social climate
- Enlist the support of interested staff from all departments
- To respond to fiscal constraints, enlist the support of volunteers, both from within and outside the institution; approach local social service agencies, colleges, and universities for their support
- Develop advisory boards composed of key staff, volunteers, and inmates and their families who will "take ownership" of the programs

In deciding whether to establish a program for incarcerated inmates and their children and what kind of program is both feasible and desirable, correctional administrators need to consider some of the concerns raised by child development specialists. The discussion here is based on conversations and correspondence with Dr. Alfred Healy of the University of Iowa Hospital School and Dr. Velma LaPoint of the National Institute of Mental Health and Howard University. Their remarks form a context for assessing strengths and weaknesses of program options presented earlier.

Physical Facilities. Physical facilities in which children of incarcerated parents might be housed are of primary importance. If the facility is a traditional prison with cellblocks and tiers of barred cells, experts generally would oppose placing children in such an environment. If, on the other hand, the facility resembles a college dormitory—as do some minimum or medium security institutions—the environment probably would be acceptable for children. If, in addition, the institution is clean, free of contagious diseases, and provides proper food, there would be no barrier to inmate mothers having their children with them.

Length of Residence. Professionals suggest that the length of the stay might be from birth (in a properly equipped and staffed nursery) up to eighteen months of age. Although there is no definite upper age limit, the frequently mentioned limit of two-years old is considered by many to be too long for a child to live at an institution. The child that age or older might be stigmatized. Officials must continually weigh what is most harmful and when intervention is appropriate. Questions regarding length of stay also depend on the length of the mother's sentence and institutional facilities. The availability of a day care center that could be operated near the institution in conjunction with the surrounding community has widespread support. Another widely supported belief is the idea that incarcerated mothers and infants should spend time together, even if the infant is in foster care placement.

Individual Considerations. Specific circumstances of each family's situation must be addressed. What, for instance, is the alternative to a particular inmate's child staying at the institution? Is it possible for the child to live with grandparents in a loving and nurturing setting or would he or she be bounced around from one foster home to another? What would be the effect of seventy-two hour, weekend, or monthly visits on the mother-child bond? Is the mother now the principal provider? Who should make decisions about placement? Foster care review boards have been proposed to study and make recommendations to the court on children already in public care. Such review boards could include individuals concerned about the children of incarcerated persons.

Special Arrangements. If infants are housed in the institution, arrangements should be made for incarcerated mothers to take responsibility for caring for their infants; for the provision of special medical equipment, if needed; for the availability of twenty-four-hour care seven days a week to the infant; for the establishment of a playroom or play area; and for monitoring the effects of the mother-child program on other female inmates. Institutions also must make some attempt to establish basic parenting norms—in other words, there should be a common understanding of the distinctions between discipline and abuse.

Prison Goals. There is continuing controversy over the purposes of imprisonment and the correctional system. Should its purpose be rehabilitation? Punishment? Incapacitation? Should the family become the center of the debate over correctional issues and philosophies? Should children be used to change the traditional notions of prison? We demonstrate our ambivalence when, on the one hand, we show adolescents through "Scared Straight" programs that prisons are ugly and dangerous but, at the same time, are willing to place innocent babies in an institution, implying, "Look how nice it is here, just like home."

Rehabilitation is a key issue in debates over programs for incarcerated mothers and their children. Advocates argue that the ability to bond and be a good mother itself is rehabilitative. Given evidence in the literature on the limited amount of rehabilitative opportunities in women's prisons, the maternal role, therefore, should be encouraged. According to Dr. LaPoint, however, "Motherhood by itself will not work magic." She also sees other dangers in residential programs for the children of incarcerated mothers:

> Within the mental health field, there is a trend toward the deinstitutionalization of certain client populations. On the other hand, within the criminal justice field, there is a trend toward institutionalization of individuals convicted of serious crimes . . . It appears contradictory to institutionalize children who have not been convicted of crimes under the rubric of the rehabilitation of mothers. Children would be subjected to a restricted form of residential living. There is another issue related to institutionalization. It may be that if facilities are made better for incarcerated mothers, who generally comprise a majority of the incarcerated women population, judicial officials may in fact begin to sentence women to institutionalized settings as opposed to probation and/or assign longer sentences in institutionalized settings.

Social Context and Alternatives. We need to understand the total context of the family, the child, the prison setting, and the society. We need to be aware of what happened prior to imprisonment. Many women had their children as teenagers and at the same time faced other crises such as limited opportunities for employment, substance abuse, and other issues, which led to criminal activity. They lacked a sense of responsibility. There are also ethnic and class differences in family functioning and child rearing. Some lower-income whites tend to use available social services agencies, while some blacks fear that by going to social service agencies they will lose their children.

Dr. Healy recommends that programs: reflect the ever-increasing emphasis on cultural diversity and all that this implies. The major component of that diversity includes family'. He suggests more research is needed on the "specific culture of the individual mother and her child." For example, he believes:

> the extremely wide range of differing family, racial, ethnic, and religious subcultures in which we as Americans exist brings a very wide latitude to the "stigma" of incarceration . . . Even ten years ago the Native American culture was only beginning to expand its primarily Midwestern/Western orientation and to impact our national thinking.

We need to address preventive measures in considering funding priorities and perhaps spend funds on services for mothers prior to their incarceration. We also need to consider alternatives to residential programs.

Dr. Healy writes:

> I support your basic concept that many of the current concerns relating to incarcerated mothers (and fathers) and their children relate to "individualized" decision-making by those who are in responsible positions within our prison systems. "Accountability" is a difficult concept to preach when salaries are low, rewards are minimal, and the characters of the players are faceless and numerous. It is so much easier to make decisions "by the book" than to attempt to place them in a human context. This is no different, however, than those in the health care or other human service fields today—make the decision and move on—your supervisor is motivated by the bottom line and not by human concerns.
>
> My comments are motivated by the feelings of a pediatrician, not as someone skilled or particularly knowledgeable of the justice system. Children need to learn love and affection, to

develop a feeling of self-worth, and to be nurtured to lead independent lives within a social context. If this can be appropriately done within a prison, let's do it—our chances are probably better within prisons than what is being often accomplished on the streets today (memo of April 24, 1996).

Similar issues arise in Britan. R. Shaw (1992c) describes some of the forces in British society and correctional institutions that result in the neglect of the needs of children of incarcerated parents. These issues are applicable to the United States and include the following:

- "Does the state have a right morally—as practice shows it has legally—to strip a child of its parent because that parent has offended, although the crime may have been less harmful to the victim than imprisonment of the offender is to his or her child? Does not the child have a right to uninterrupted parenting at least equal to the right of the state to punish?"
- How are we to "achieve a more humane and responsible balance between the rights of the prisoner and the need for security on the one side and the rights and needs of the child for a meaningful relationship with the imprisoned mother or father on the other?"
- "Home leaves" (furloughs) granted early in a sentence can help maintain the parent/child relationship without "presenting logistic difficulties and pressure on space" that might result from "a big expansion of visits or the introduction of conjugal visits."
- "Recent changes in social security legislation" (in Britain), and proposed changes in the United States dealing with welfare reform, social security, Medicare, and Medicaid, "hit hardest at those at the very bottom of the social ladder and cuts in family planning, infant welfare foods, health visiting services, to name but a few, has very serious implications for families and again hit hardest at those on the bottom line—and that means the majority of prisoners' children. The rest of society is also hit when it has to pick up the pieces."
- Crime prevention policies and programs are needed "to reduce crime at its origin instead of spending vast sums of money dealing with its aftermath."

Other issues include the following concerns:

As female patterns of interaction with the criminal justice system become quantitatively more similar to male patterns, mother-child reunification among women offenders is decreasing, terminations of their parental rights are increasing, and we are seeing a greater number of women prisoners who, like men, did not live with their children prior to incarceration and will probably not live with them after release. This is not happening because women offenders are assuming what appear to be male patterns of parenting, but rather because the dissolution of the family is the consequence of repeated parental incarcerations. Such circumstances require, perhaps as a first priority, services for incarcerated parents that address not only prearrest and postrelease reunification issues, but also the prevention of recidivism (Johnston and Gabel 1995).

"In light of the poor economic situations faced by most administrators of state prisons for women" the following recommendations may be possible:

Community-based services that network with a facility's administration could provide many of the counseling, teaching, and advising services for pregnant inmates. The best type of facility presently available to provide the necessary care for pregnant inmates may be the halfway house. As suggested by McHugh (1980), legislation should be enacted that requires that pregnant women be housed in separate facilities that specifically address the special needs of this population (Wooldredge and Masters 1993).

Johnston (1995) summarizes the key issues that she believes need to be addressed. These include providing more research and program evaluation, dealing with parental recidivism, changing correctional policies and procedures, and addressing the problem of poverty. Based on these issues, our society is challenged to examine the lives of children in trouble more thoroughly and to disseminate research findings widely and more quickly.

> For if compulsive behaviors and criminal activity represent relatively resilient responses to life in poor, violent, chaotic families and neighborhoods, then our society is condemned to incarcerating an ever-increasing number of the people who live in these circumstances, unless we can help them to reduce the poverty, violence, and chaos in their lives.

Recommendations

For humanitarian and moral reasons, more can be done for inmates' children and their families. The extent to which infants and young children can be cared for at correctional institutions must be decided on the basis of the amount of funds a state is willing to commit to such programs and individual institutional circumstances.

In some cases, a child's best option may be to remain with his or her mother in a correctional institution, particularly when placement with other family members is not possible. The placement decision should be decided on case-by-case basis by regional foster care review boards (Brodie 1982; the consensus of Iowa pediatricians, *Wainright v. Moore*, 374 So. 2nd 586, Florida District Court of Appeals, 1979).

The reasons for discontinuing prison nurseries seem to have been administrative or political ones. There is no research evidence indicating their abandonment was related in any way to the programs' benefits or lack of

benefits to children, inmates, or the institution. It may be useful, therefore, to reinstate previously existing programs. With appropriate funding and support, they may yet prove worthwhile. This is as true of prison nurseries as of penal colonies. Without adequate research and evaluation we will never know. Given the experience of several states with prison nurseries, a valuable retrospective study could be made of former prison mothers and children who lived with them in correctional institutions in Florida, Illinois, Kansas, Massachusetts, New York, and Virginia.

The state of Iowa has had legislation since 1967 authorizing the use of work release for incarcerated mothers to care for their children and families. In 1974, the law was expanded to include incarcerated fathers. Greater use of such statutes, in Iowa as well as in other states, should be considered to maintain the family unit.

Programs for incarcerated parents and their families require a clearer commitment on the part of correctional professionals and legislators regarding the goals of corrections. Traditional ideological conflicts among advocates of security/control, punishment, revenge, retribution, deterrence, reintegration, or rehabilitation have negative consequences for the inmate and his or her family. Their resolution is not likely to come from higher mountains of rhetoric, but from the willingness of decision makers and policy makers to be more open-minded and supportive of the scientific evaluation of their policies and programs.

Some of the evaluation issues raised by Powell (1994) and others include:

- randomization—whether this is ethically possible
- how to define and measure quality, success, and outcomes
- qualitative versus quantitative measures
- methodological issues
- whether evaluation is a scientific or political endeavor, or a combination of both
- short term versus long-term effects

In 1976, Boudouris emphasized accountability. In 1984, he argued for the development of the right programs for the right offenders to reduce recidivism. In 1988, Boudouris and others called for collaboration. Another author, Christie (1994), describes annual conferences of Scandinavian academicians, correctional officials, criminologists, inmates, and other concerned individuals during which issues are discussed and plans for reform are introduced. No such collaborative efforts take place in the United States, except for the American Correctional Association conferences that are held twice each year.

Margaret Shaw (1992) describes some of the problems that may result even under the best conditions for collaborative efforts, based on the activities of the "Task Force for Federally Sentenced Women" that was set up in 1989 in Canada. The Task Force conducted a survey of all federally sentenced women; of 203 women, only twenty-five refused to participate. It is described as an "important landmark in the transformation of women's imprisonment."

However, the transformation may be fraught with danger:

- The issue of whose "knowledge" is valid may raise problems. Examples are given where the task force's report does not represent what the inmates "actually want . . . "
- (W)hile many women indicated that they had considerable experience with alcohol and drugs, this cannot be taken to imply that they either need or are ready for treatment programmes." Shaw adds, "It is too easy to blame the women for being 'unwilling to confront their problems' when in many cases the blame belongs with inadequacies in the provision of programmes."
- The task force represents "a feminist vision" but it is selective in its listening. "While it responds to the women's need to exercise control over their lives, at the same time, . . . it seems to deny that they are capable of making choices." Shaw relates this to an image of the women as victims and in a "childlike" status, and she emphasizes that "the plurality of their views needs to be recognized."
- The task force "places a strong emphasis on the women's need for self-esteem," and yet, "not one of the women interviewed said that they wanted programmes on self-esteem. These are needs as defined by others . . . "
- "(T)here is the problem of oversimplification, of assuming that the 'current' explanation applies to all women."

Shaw concludes, "In our efforts to defend the women in prison, the defenders run the risk of substituting male paternalism with what could be seen as 'feminist-paternalism'."

5. Table: Institutional Programs for Incarcerated Mothers and Their Children

This comprehensive table presents a state-by-state illustration of seven types of programs for inmate mothers and their children. It includes: prison nurseries, overnight stays, family and conjugal visits, children's and day care centers, parenting classes, furloughs, and community facilities. It also identifies the specific institutions and programs surveyed in this study, as well as the number of female prisoners held in the facilities at the time of the survey (December 1995 to April 1996). Note: federal facilities are included in the state where they are located.

RESOURCES

Programs for Incarcerated Mothers and Their Children

State and Number of Female Inmates Surveyed	*Prison Nurseries*	*Overnight Visits with Children*	*Family Visits/ Conjugal Visits*	*Children's and Day Care Centers*	*Parenting Classes for Inmates*	*Furloughs*	*Community Facilities for Mothers and Children*	*Institutions and Other Programs*
AK (66)	No	No	No	No	No	No	No	Meadow Creek Women's Facility Eagle River
AL (800)	No	No	Family: Yes Conjugal: No	No	Yes	No	No	Julia Tutwiler Prison for Women Wetumpka *A.I.M., Inc. (Aid to Inmate Mothers)*
AR (526)	No	No	No	No	Yes	Yes	No	Tucker Unit for Women Tucker
AZ (412)	No	No	No	No	Yes	No	No	Arizona State Prison Complex-Perryville Goodyear
AZ (435)	No	No	Family: Yes Conjugal: No	No	Yes	No	No	Arizona State Prison Complex-Phoenix Phoenix
AZ (214)	No	No	Family: Yes: Conjugal: No	Yes	Yes	Yes	No	Federal Satellite Camp Phoenix
AZ (32)	No	No	Family: Yes: Conjugal: No	Yes	Yes	Yes	No	Federal Correctional Institution Tucson

RESOURCES

Programs for Incarcerated Mothers and Their Children

State and Number of Female Inmates Surveyed	*Prison Nurseries*	*Overnight Visits with Children*	*Family Visits/ Conjugal Visits*	*Children's and Day Care Centers*	*Parenting Classes for Inmates*	*Furloughs*	*Community Facilities for Mothers and Children*	*Institutions and Other Programs*
CA (1,124)	No	No	Family: Yes: Conjugal: No	Yes	Yes	Yes	No	Federal Correctional Institution & Satellite Camp Dublin
CA (2,935)	No	Yes	Yes	No	Yes	No	Yes	Central Calif. Women's Facility Chowchilla *Prisoner Mother-Infant Program* *Las Comadres Program* *Amer-I-Can Self-Esteem Program* *Friends Outside* *Community Prisoner Mother Program (CPMP)*
CA (793)	No	Yes	Yes	No	Yes	No	Yes	Northern Calif. Stockton Women's Facility *Las Comadres Program* *Community Prisoner Mother Program (CPMP)*
CA (2,300)	No	Yes	Yes	No	Yes	Yes	Yes	Valley State Prison for Women Chowchilla *Las Comadres Program* *Community Prisoner Mother Program (CPMP)*
CA (1,739)	No	Yes	Yes	No	Yes	Yes	Yes	California Institute for Women Frontera *Las Comadres Program* *Community Prisoner Mother Program (CPMP)*
CA (803)	No	Yes	Yes	No	Yes	Yes	Yes	California Rehabilitation Center Norco *Las Comadres Program* *Community Prisoner Mother Program (CPMP)*
CA (327)	No	Yes	Yes	No	Yes	Yes	Yes	Sierra Conservation Center Jamestown *Las Comadres Program* *Community Prisoner Mother Program (CPMP)*

RESOURCES

Programs for Incarcerated Mothers and Their Children

State and Number of Female Inmates Surveyed	*Prison Nurseries*	*Overnight Visits with Children*	*Family Visits/ Conjugal Visits*	*Children's and Day Care Centers*	*Parenting Classes for Inmates*	*Furloughs*	*Community Facilities for Mothers and Children*	*Institutions and Other Programs*
CO (260)	No	No	No	No	Yes	No	No	Women's Correctional Facility Canon City *Mennonites' Program (Foster Care)*
CT (1,103)	No	FPC Only	Family: Yes Conjugal: No	Yes	Yes	FPC Only	No	Federal Corr. Institution and Prison Camp (FPC) Danbury *Children's Center* *Family Literacy Programs* *Parents Anonymous*
CT (450)	No	Yes	Yes	Yes	Yes	Yes	Yes	Connecticut Correctional Institution Niantic *Parenting Program* *Creative Arts Program/Sesame Street Visiting*
DC (210)	No	No	No	No	Yes	No	No	Correctional Treatment Facility District of Columbia *Parenting and Literacy Skills (PALS) Program*
DE (265)	Proposed	Yes	Family: Yes Conjugal: No	No	Yes	No	No	Delores J. Baylor Women's Correctional Institution New Castle *Project Reconnect*
FL (401)	No	No	Family: Yes: Conjugal: No	Yes	Yes	Yes	No	Federal Correctional Institution & Satellite Camp Marianna
FL (601)	No	No	Family: Yes Conjugal: No	No	Yes	Yes (Death bed & Funerals)	No	Broward Correctional Institution Pembroke Pines *Girl Scouts Beyond Bars* *"Even Start" - Family Literacy Program*
FL (1,311)	No	No	Family: Yes Conjugal: No	No	Yes	Yes	No	Florida Correctional Institution Forest Hills Unit & Levy Camp Lowell *Pregnancy Furlough* *Parenting Education*

RESOURCES

Programs for Incarcerated Mothers and Their Children

State and Number of Female Inmates Surveyed	*Prison Nurseries*	*Overnight Visits with Children*	*Family Visits/ Conjugal Visits*	*Children's and Day Care Centers*	*Parenting Classes for Inmates*	*Furloughs*	*Community Facilities for Mothers and Children*	*Institutions and Other Programs*
FL (748)	No	No	Family: Yes Conjugal: No	No	Yes	Yes (Death bed & Funerals)	No	Jefferson Correctional Institution Monticello *RITE* *Diversified Coop. Training (DCT)* *AA/NA*
GA (750)	No	No	Family: *Yes* Conjugal: No	Yes	Yes	No	No	Metro Correctional Institution Atlanta *Project REACH*
HI (110)	No	No	No	Yes	Yes	Yes	No	Women's Community Kailua Correctional Center *Kid's Day (on weekends)*
IA (350)	No	No	Family: *Yes* Conjugal: No	No	Yes	Yes	Yes	Correctional Institution for Women Mitchellville *Prison Fellowship*
ID (161)	No	No (Extended visits planned)	Family: Yes Conjugal: No	No	Yes	Yes	No	Pocatello Women's Correctional Center Pocatello *Holiday Party (5-Hour Extended Visit)*
IL (260)	No	No	Family: Yes: Conjugal: No	Yes	Yes	Yes	No	Federal Satellite Camp Pekin
IL (695)	No	Yes	Family: Yes Conjugal: No	Yes	Yes	No	No	Dwight Correctional Center Dwight *Camp Celebration* *Motherlove Parenting Classes*
IL (195)	No	Yes	Family: *Yes* Conjugal: No	Yes	Yes	No	No	Kankakee MSU Manteno *Camp Celebration* *Motherlove Parenting Classes*

RESOURCES

Programs for Incarcerated Mothers and Their Children

State and Number of Female Inmates Surveyed	*Prison Nurseries*	*Overnight Visits with Children*	*Family Visits / Conjugal Visits*	*Children's and Day Care Centers*	*Parenting Classes for Inmates*	*Furloughs*	*Community Facilities for Mothers and Children*	*Institutions and Other Programs*
IN (400)	No	No	No	Planned	Yes	No	Yes	Indiana Women's Prison Indianapolis *Family Preservation Center (proposed)* *Parents in Touch Program* *YWCA Incarcerated Mothers Program* *Support Groups*
KS (443)	No	Yes	Family: Yes Conjugal: No	Yes	Yes	Yes	Yes	Topeka Correctional Facility Women's Activities Learning Center (WALC) Topeka *Dads and Their Dependents (DADS)* *Inmate Family Integration Services (IFRS)* *Prep. for Drug-Free Years* *United Methodist Women Volunteers*
KY (465)	No	Yes	Family: Yes Conjugal: No	No	Yes	Yes	Yes	KY Corr. Institution for Women Pewce Valley *"Bonding Room"* *"Kid's Day" and "Teen Day"*
LA (720)	No	No	Family: Yes Conjugal: No	No	Yes	Yes	No	Louisiana Correctional Institution for Women St. Gabriel *"Caring Parents"* *Children's Day at Easter and Christmas*
MA (564)	No	No	Family: Yes Conjugal: No	Yes	Yes	No	No	Massachusetts Correctional Institution Framingham *Girl Scouts Beyond Bars: ACCESS Program* *"Catch the Hope" Perinatal Clinic* *Parents Anonymous* *A.I.M. (Aid to Incarcerated Mothers)* *WINAS (Women In Need of Alternate Solutions)*

RESOURCES

Programs for Incarcerated Mothers and Their Children

State and Number of Female Inmates Surveyed	*Prison Nurseries*	*Overnight Visits with Children*	*Family Visits / Conjugal Visits*	*Children's and Day Care Centers*	*Parenting Classes for Inmates*	*Furloughs*	*Community Facilities for Mothers and Children*	*Institutions and Other Programs*
MA (56)	No	Yes	Family: Yes Conjugal: No	No	Yes	Yes (Emerg. & Funerals)	Yes	Lancaster Pre-Release Center Lancaster *A.I.M. (Aid to Incarcerated Mothers)*
MD (159)	No	Yes	Yes	No	Yes	Yes	Yes	Baltimore Pre-Release Unit-Women Jessup *House of Ruth*
MD (48)	No	Yes	Family: Yes Conjugal: No	No	Yes	No	No	Patuxent Institution for Women Jessup *Developing Parent / Child Therapy Grp*
ME (40)	No	No	No	No	Yes	Yes	No	Maine Correctional Center Windham *Parents Helping Incarcerated (HIP)*
MI (820)	No	No	No	No	Yes	No	Yes	Scott Correctional Facility Plymouth *Childrens Visitation Program (CVP)* *Project Transition (Residential Facility in Detroit)*
MI (449)	No	No	Family: Yes Conjugal: No	No	Yes	No	No	Florence Crane Women's Facility Coldwater *Kids Need Moms, Inc.*
MI (304)	No	No	No	No	Yes	Limited	No	Camp Branch Coldwater
MN (200)	No	Yes	Family: Yes Conjugal: No	No	Yes	Yes	Yes	Minnesota Correctional Facility Shakopee *Roosevelt Parenting Unit* *Parenting Teens* *Parenting With Pride* *Baby Ready / Baby Steps* *CAMP / ReEntry / Genesis II* *Odyssey Group* *Project HOPE*

RESOURCES

Programs for Incarcerated Mothers and Their Children

State and Number of Female Inmates Surveyed	*Prison Nurseries*	*Overnight Visits with Children*	*Family Visits/ Conjugal Visits*	*Children's and Day Care Centers*	*Parenting Classes for Inmates*	*Furloughs*	*Community Facilities for Mothers and Children*	*Institutions and Other Programs*
MO (650)	No	No	No	Yes	Yes	No	No	Chillicothe Correctional Center Chillicothe *PATCH Prog. (Parents & Their Children)* *Agape House for visiting families*
MO (350)	No	No	No	Yes	Yes	Yes	No	Renz Correctional Center Jefferson City *PATCH Prog. (Parents & Their Children)*
MS (575)	No	Yes	Yes	Planned	Planned	No	Yes	Central Mississippi Correctional Facility Pearl *(Parenting program in planning stage)* *Furloughs from Community Work Center*
MT (65)	No	Yes	No	No	Yes	No	No	Women's Correctional Center Warm Springs
NC (263)	No	No	Family: Yes Conjugal: No	Yes	Yes	Yes	No	Federal Satellite Camp Butner
NC (26)	No	No	Family: Yes Conjugal: No	No	No	No	No	Wilmington Residential Facility for Women Wilmington
NC (980)	No	Overnight: No Extended: Yes	Family: Yes Conjugal: No	Yes	Yes	Yes	Yes	Correctional Institution for Women Raleigh Harriet House; Summit House *MATCH (Mothers and Their Children)* *STEP Parenting Program* *Motheread Program*
NC (500)	No	No	No	No	No	Yes	No	Fountain Correctional Center Rocky Mount
ND (40)	No	No	No	No	Yes	No	No	North Dakota State Penitentiary Bismarck

RESOURCES

Programs for Incarcerated Mothers and Their Children

State and Number of Female Inmates Surveyed	*Prison Nurseries*	*Overnight Visits with Children*	*Family Visits/ Conjugal Visits*	*Children's and Day Care Centers*	*Parenting Classes for Inmates*	*Furloughs*	*Community Facilities for Mothers and Children*	*Institutions and Other Programs*
NE (135)	Yes	Yes	No	No	Yes	No	No	Nebraska Center for Women York *Nursery Program* *Project M.O.L.D. (Mother Offspring Life Development)*
NH (77)	No	Overnight: No Extended: New Mothers	Family: Yes Conjugal: No	Yes	Yes	No	Yes	New Hampshire State Prison for Women Goffstown
NJ (880)	No	No	Yes	No	Yes	Yes	No	Edna Mahan Correctional Facility Clinton *Girl Scouting Behind Bars* *Mother-Child Visitation*
NM (286)	No	Yes	Yes	No	Yes	Yes	No	Women's Correctional Facility Grants *Peanut Butter & Jelly Prog. (ImPACT)* *Children's Day Parties*
NV (130)	No	No	Family: Yes Conjugal: No	No	Yes	No	No	Silver Springs Conservation Camp Silver Springs *AA/NA*
NV (250)	No	No	No	No	Yes	No	No	Women's Correctional Center Carson City *Bradshaw & the Family*
NY (760)	Yes	Yes	Yes	Yes	Yes	Yes	Yes	Bedford Hills Correctional Facility Bedford Hills *Family Reunion Program* *Children's Center* *Providence House for parolees* *My Mother's House (foster home for children)*
NY (500)	Yes	No	No	Yes	Yes	Yes	Yes	Taconic Correctional Facility Bedford Hills *Comprehensive Alcohol and Substance Abuse Treatment (CASAT)*

RESOURCES

Programs for Incarcerated Mothers and Their Children

State and Number of Female Inmates Surveyed	*Prison Nurseries*	*Overnight Visits with Children*	*Family Visits/ Conjugal Visits*	*Children's and Day Care Centers*	*Parenting Classes for Inmates*	*Furloughs*	*Community Facilities for Mothers and Children*	*Institutions and Other Programs*
OH (495)	No	No	Family: Yes Conjugal: No	No	Yes	No	No	Franklin Pre-Release Center Columbus *Prenatal Program* *Girl Scouts Beyond Bars* *Juvenile Justice Program*
OH (1,578)	No	Yes	Family: Yes Conjugal: No	No	Yes	No	No	Ohio Reformatory for Women Marysville *STEP Parenting Program* *Girl Scouts Beyond Bars* *Camp Adventures Mom and Me* *Visiting Hall Crafts Project*
OK (334)	No	Yes	Family: Yes Conjugal: No	No	Yes	No	No	Mabel Bassett Corr. Center Oklahoma City *CAMP (Children & Mother's Program)*
OR (241)	No	Overnight: No Extended: Yes	Family: Yes Conjugal: No	No	Yes	No	No	Columbia River Correctional Institution Portland *Turning Point (ASAP Program)* *Family Learning Circle (Literacy Program)* *WICS*
OR (178)	No	No	Family: Yes Conjugal: No	No	Yes	No	Yes	Oregon Women's Correctional Center Salem *Recovery In Focus*
PA (885)	No	No	No	Yes	Yes	Yes	Yes	State Correctional Institution at Muncy *Project IMPACT*
PA (530)	No	No	No	Planned	Yes	Yes	No	State Correctional Institution at Cambridge Springs Cambridge Springs *Parenting Program* *WINGS for Kids* *(Women Inside Needing Guidance and Support)*

RESOURCES

Programs for Incarcerated Mothers and Their Children

State and Number of Female Inmates Surveyed	*Prison Nurseries*	*Overnight Visits with Children*	*Family Visits/ Conjugal Visits*	*Children's and Day Care Centers*	*Parenting Classes for Inmates*	*Furloughs*	*Community Facilities for Mothers and Children*	*Institutions and Other Programs*
RI (146)	No	Yes	No	Yes	Yes	Yes	No	Women's Facilities Cranston *Student Interns*
SC (382)	No	No	Family: Yes Conjugal: No	No	Yes	No	No	Leath Correctional Institution - Women Greenwood *Parenting from a Distance* *Mothers' Reading Program*
SC (365)	No	No	Family: Yes Conjugal: No	No	Yes	No	No	Women's Correctional Institution Columbia
SD (120)	No	Yes	Family: Yes Conjugal: No	No	Yes	Minimum *Status*	No	Springfield State Prison Springfield Parents and Children Together (PACT) *Mother-Infant Program*
TN (20)	No	No	Family: Yes Conjugal: No	No	Yes	After	No	Chattanooga Community Service Parole Center Chattanooga
TX (721)	No	No	No	Yes	Yes	Yes	Yes	Federal Prison Camp & ICC Bryan Mothers & Infants Together Parenting Center
TX (500)	No	Yes	Family: Yes Conjugal: No	No	Yes	Yes	No	Lockhart Correctional Facility Lockart (Privately run by Wackenhut Corrections)
UT (161)	No	No	Family: Yes Conjugal: No	No	Yes	No	No	Utah State Prison-Olympus Facility, Draper
UT (29)	No	No	Family: Yes Conjugal: No	No	Yes	No	No	Women's Pre-Release Facility Draper (Privately run by Management Training Corp., Ogden)

RESOURCES

Programs for Incarcerated Mothers and Their Children

State and Number of Female Inmates Surveyed	*Prison Nurseries*	*Overnight Visits with Children*	*Family Visits/ Conjugal Visits*	*Children's and Day Care Centers*	*Parenting Classes for Inmates*	*Furloughs*	*Community Facilities for Mothers and Children*	*Institutions and Other Programs*
VA (741)	No	No	Family: Yes Conjugal: No	No	Yes	No	No	Virginia Correctional Center for Women Goochland *MILK (Mothers Inside Loving Kids)*
VT (40)	No	No	Family: Yes Conjugal: No	No	Yes	No	No	Chittenden Regional Correctional Facility South Burlington
WA (508)	No	Yes	Yes	Yes	Yes	No	No	Washington Corr. Center for Women Gig Harbor
WI (329)	No	Yes	Family: Yes Conjugal: No	No	Yes	No	No	Taycheedah Correctional Institute Fond du Lac *Extended Visitation*
WV (670)	No	No	Family: Yes: Conjugal: No	Yes	Yes	Yes	No	Federal Satellite Camp Alderson
WV (10)	No	Overnight: No Extended: Yes	Family: Yes Conjugal: No	No	Yes	Yes	No	Charleston Work/Study Release Center Charleston
WY (83)	No	No	No	No	Yes	Yes	No	Wyoming Women's Center Lusk
CANADA								
Manitoba (44)	Yes	Yes	No	No	Yes	Yes	No	Portage Correctional Institution *AA/Substance Abuse Program* *"Babies Behind Bars"* *"Abuse Hurts" Program* *Native Culture Program*
Newfndland (7)	No	Overnight: No Extended: Yes	Family: Yes Conjugal: No	No	Yes	Yes	No, but possible	Nfld. & Labrador Corr. Centre for Women Stephenville
Ontario (130)	No	Yes	Yes	No	Yes	Yes	No	Prison for Women Kingston

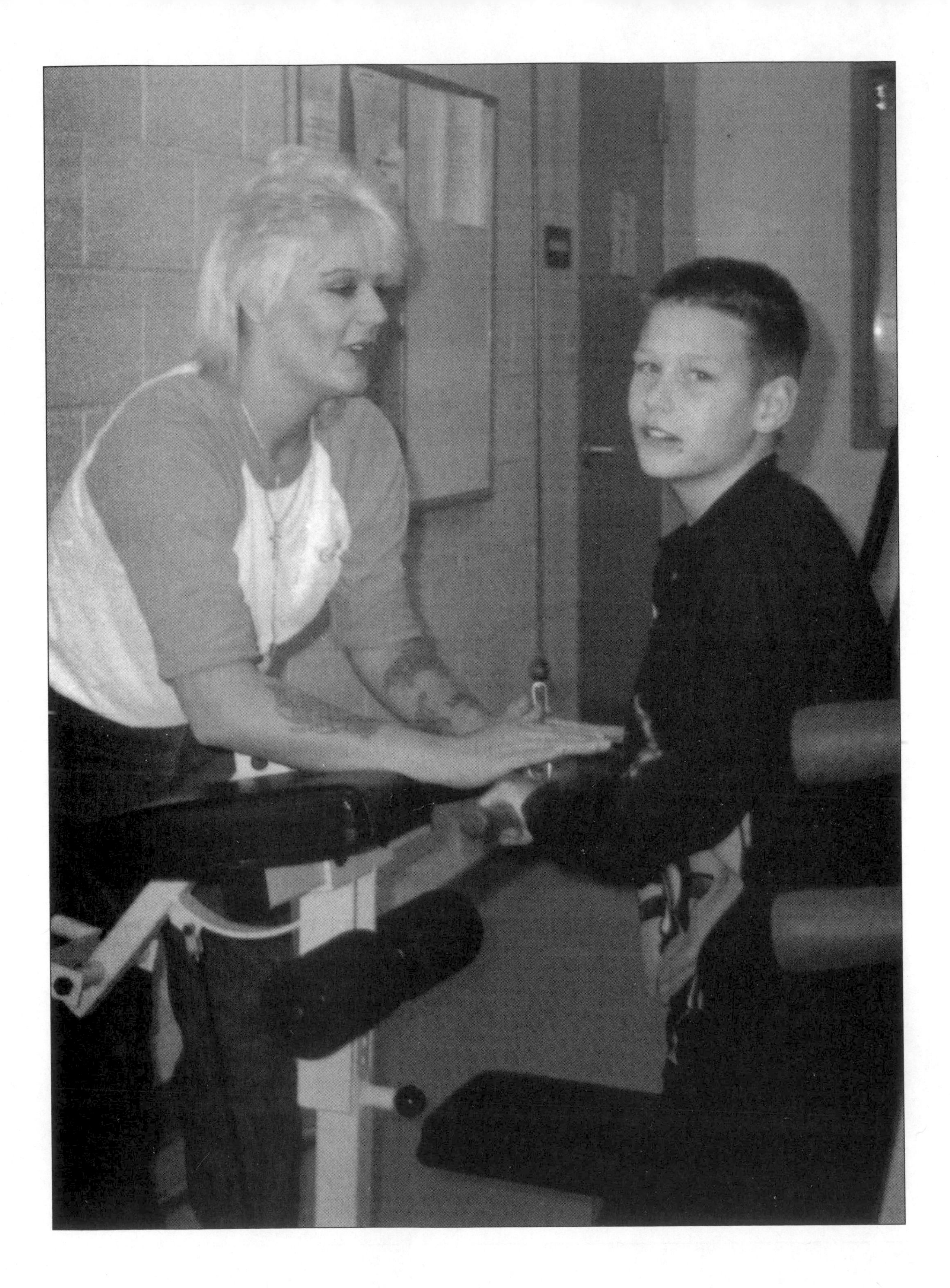

6. Policies

American Correctional Association - Public Correctional Policy on Female Offender Services - 1995

This policy was unanimously ratified by the American Correctional Association Delegate Assembly at the 114th Congress of Correction, in San Antonio, Texas on August 23, 1984. It was reviewed in 1990 with no change, and it was adopted as amended on August 9, 1995 at the 125th Congress of Correction in Cincinnati, Ohio.

Correctional systems must develop service delivery systems for accused and adjudicated female offenders that are comparable to those provided to males. Additional services must also be provided to meet the unique needs of the female offender population.

Policy Statement:

Correctional systems must be guided by the principle of parity. Female offenders must receive the equivalent range of services available to other offenders, including opportunities for individualized programming and services that recognize the unique needs of this population. The services should:

A. Assure access to a range of alternatives to incarceration, including pre-trial and post-trial diversion, probation, restitution, treatment for substance abuse, halfway houses, and parole services;

B. Provide acceptable conditions of confinement, including appropriately trained staff and sound operating procedures that address this population's needs in such areas as clothing, personal property, hygiene, exercise, recreation, and visitations with children and family;

C. Provide access to a full range of work and programs designed to expand economic and social roles of women, with emphasis on education; career counseling and exploration of nontraditional vocational training; relevant life skills, including parenting and social and economic assertiveness; and pre-release and work/education release programs;

D. Facilitate the maintenance and strengthening of family ties, particularly those between parent and child;

E. Deliver appropriate programs and services, including medical, dental, and mental health programs, services to pregnant women, substance abuse programs, child and family services, and provide access to legal services, and

F. Provide access to release programs that include aid in achieving economic stability and the development of supportive family relationships.

Federal Bureau of Prison's Policy Statement. (Parenting Program Standard - #5355.03 - January 20, 1995)

Correctional administrators considering or planning programs for inmate parents and their children may want to refer to this standard for guidance. It represents a response to the issues confronting institutions seeking to preserve their inmates' parental relationships.

Purpose and Scope. To provide standards for parenting programs in all institutions.

Beginning in 1986, the United States congressional appropriations conference reports for the Bureau included recommended parenting program funding levels. Initially, funding was provided at four female institutions and subsequently at all female institutions and at least one male institution in each BOP region. Conference reports also identified appropriate visiting room space, parent education, social service outreach, and community based service providers as desirable parenting program characteristics. This Program Statement expands such programs to all institutions.

Program Objectives. The expected results of this program are:

a. Positive relationships, family values, and mutual support and nurturing, which may be sustained after release, will be promoted and reinforced among inmates and their spouses and children.
b. Each inmate will have opportunities to counteract negative family consequences resulting from his/her incarceration.
c. The institutional social environment will be improved through opportunities for inmates to maintain positive and sustaining contact with their families.
d. Social service and community based organizations will be included in parenting programs whenever possible.

Program Scope.

a. Parenting programs shall be established in all institutions housing Federal prisoners.
b. The program shall be under the general guidance of the Education Department, and a specific staff member in that department shall be assigned to coordinate and monitor the program. Cooperation and coordination between Education staff and other departments shall be established, with specific emphasis on building strong liaison with the Psychology Services and Chaplaincy Departments. Parenting programs may be offered during evening hours and/or weekends if local conditions warrant.

   Any institution, which because of its special mission or population requires a waiver from all or part(s) of this Program Statement, shall seek a waiver in accordance with the Program Statement, Directives Management Manual.
c. Parenting program funds shall be provided, whenever available, through regional allocations for each institution. Funding levels shall be adequate to meet established standards and to provide quality programs.

Program Standards. All programs shall include the following:

a. Visiting Space. Space shall be provided for each program. While separate space is preferred, if this is not possible, a section of the institution's visiting room shall be reserved for the parenting program. Institutions which designate separate space for this program shall, when possible, establish visiting hours coinciding with regular visiting room hours. Staff shall at all times adhere to local visiting room policies and procedures.

b. Social Services. Wherever possible, social services outreach contacts shall be established with community-based social service organizations to facilitate the provision of services to the inmate parent, visiting custodial parent, and children. Social services, as defined, are services provided to promote and enhance human welfare. These services may include assistance in such areas as veterans' benefits, welfare support, child care, health promotion and disease prevention, prenatal and postnatal care, etc.

Program coordinators, in coordination with institution volunteer coordinators, are encouraged to use community-based volunteers and appropriate organizations, whenever possible. These services may include, but are not limited to, such organizations as: Boy\Girl Scouts, Boys and Girls Clubs of America, Children's Television Workshop (CTW), Literacy Volunteers of America (LVA), and local colleges and universities.

c. Parenting Education. A parenting education component, as described [below], shall be offered in each parenting program.

Parenting Education Program Outline. The following is a "recommended" program outline for the parenting education component of the program.

a. Parenting Skills.
   (1) Building or continuing family relationships while incarcerated, including the use of community support systems;
   (2) Accomplishing age-appropriate communication with children during long periods of absence, including explaining a parent's incarceration to children;
   (3) Engaging in interactive play with children during visiting;
   (4) Recognizing and contributing to the stages of childhood development, including proper nutrition;
   (5) Administering appropriate and effective discipline;
   (6) Fostering self-esteem in children;
   (7) Participating in a child's education process;
   (8) Preventing childhood injuries, including physical and sexual abuse;
   (9) Dealing with sibling rivalry; and
   (10) Identifying factors that indicate personal readiness for parenthood, including knowledge of a positive environment for children.

b. Skills for Family Support.
   (1) Analyzing family needs and determining how those needs can be met;
   (2) Managing a family budget;
   (3) Developing skills to cope with change; increasing stress management skills; and
   (4) Setting priorities, and obtaining problem solving techniques.

c. Family Literacy Education.
   (1) Understanding the importance of raising the reading levels of inmates, spouses, and their children;
   (2) Motivating family interest in literacy, e.g., reading to each other, watching and discussing interactive TV programs, including the use of reading materials;
   (3) Organizing and developing a time

frame to assist children with reading, writing, homework, etc;

(4) Developing effective tutoring skills; and

(5) Compiling a list of education resources to assist in family literacy for the inmate and family members while incarcerated and after release.

d. Substance Abuse Education.

(1) Explaining the effects of parental use of addictive substances on children;

(2) Discussing components of the addictive personality;

(3) Introducing strategies to break substance addiction; and

(4) Organizing support groups.

e. Prenatal Care Information for Expectant Mothers.

(1) Achieving and/or maintaining physical fitness;

(2) Developing and/or maintaining a proper diet;

(3) Evaluating childbirth procedure options; and

(4) Providing appropriate infant care.

Record Keeping Each parenting program shall maintain records to include the following information:

a. A full description of the program scope, including room/child care center space provided, the names of social services accessed, the service provided, and related information.

b. Amount of funds spent on the program during the fiscal year including estimated value of "free services," overhead cost, (estimated at 20 percent, if actual figures are not available), value of BOP staff time, materials used, and related items.

c. Nonduplicated number of inmate parent enrollments and completions in each structured parenting class, the number of hours per week, the number of weeks per year, per enrollee, and totals for the fiscal year.

d. Nonduplicated number of children involved in the program and the number of hours of involvement per child per year, and total for the fiscal year.

e. A copy of all curriculums used in parenting education and related courses.

Non-English-Proficient Inmates. In the administration and implementation of this Program Statement, and in accordance with the Program Statement on Education, Training and Leisure Time Program Standards, efforts shall be made to meet the needs of non-English-proficient inmates and their visiting spouses and children.

Service Providers. The method for providing parenting program services, as specifically adapted to each institution, are at each institution's discretion, either through services provided by incumbent full-time staff, through procurement procedures, or a combination of both. Community-based nonprofit organizations shall be given consideration as service providers.

Procurement Procedures. The scope of work used in requests for proposals for parenting programs shall specify all the relevant required program standards outlined in this Program Statement.

Program Evaluation. The Program Review Division shall monitor compliance with this Program Statement during regularly scheduled program reviews.

Uniform Law Commissioners' Model Sentencing and Corrections Act - 1979

Correctional administrators considering or planning programs for inmate parents and their children may want to refer to the model act for guidance. It represents a thoughtful attempt to respond to the issues confronting institutions seeking to preserve their inmates' parental relationships.

Section 4-116 (Preserving Parental Relationships.)

A. The director shall:

1. assist confined persons in (i) communicating with their children and otherwise keeping informed of their affairs, and (ii) participating in decisions relating to the custody, care, and instruction of their children; and
2. provide any confined person or any person accused of an offense access to relevant information about child-care facilities available in the department, counseling, and other assistance in order to aid the person in making arrangements for his child.

B. The director may:

1. establish and maintain facilities or parts of facilities suitable for the care and housing of confined persons with their children;
2. authorize periodic extended or overnight visits by children with a confined person;
3. authorize a child, upon the request of the confined person, to reside with the person in a facility while the person is entitled to custody of the child or if the person gives birth to the child during confinement.

C. In determining whether a child may reside in a facility or visit a facility on an extended or overnight basis pursuant to subsection (B), the following factors, among others, must be considered:
1. the best interest of the child and the confined person;
2. the length of sentence imposed on the confined person and the likelihood that the child could remain in the facility throughout the confined person's term;
3. the nature and extent of suitable facilities within the department;
4. available alternatives that would protect and strengthen the relationship between the child and the confined person; and
5. the age of the child.

D. A child may not reside in a facility or visit a facility on an extended or overnight basis if:
1. the division of correctional medical services certifies that the confined person is physically or emotionally unable to care for the child;
2. the (Department of Welfare) certifies that the conditions in the facility will result in a substantial detriment to the physical or emotional well-being of the child; or
3. the (juvenile, family court) orders that the child not do so.

E. Whenever a child is authorized to reside in facility or visit a facility on an extended or overnight basis, the director shall provide for the child's basic needs including food, clothing, and medical care if the confined person is unable to do so. The department is subrogated to any rights the confined person has against any other person or organization on account of those expenses.

F. Whenever the director allows a child to reside with a confined person in a facility he shall notify the (Department of Welfare) which may take any action authorized by law to protect the best interest of the child.

G. This section does not limit or otherwise affect the power of a court to determine the nature and extent of parental rights of confined persons or to determine the custody of children.

7. References

Adalist-Estrin, A. 1994. Family Support and Criminal Justice. In S. L. Kagan and B. Weissbourd, eds. *Putting Families First: America's Family Support Movement and the Challenge of Change.* San Francisco: Jossey-Bass.

___.1995. Strengthening Inmate-Family Relationships: Programs That Work. *Corrections Today.* December.

Ainsworth, M. D. S. 1973. The Development of Mother-Infant Attachment. In B. M. Caldwell and H. N. Ricciute, eds. Review of *Child Development Research.* Chicago: University of Chicago Press.

American Correctional Association. 1981. *The Mexican Penal Colony at Islas Marias: Implications for Alternative Environments for Long-Term Incarcer-ation.* College Park, MD: American Correctional Association.

___. 1995. Public Correctional Policy on Female Offender Services.

___. 1996. *Directory of Juvenile and Adult Correctional Departments, Institutions, Agencies and Paroling Authorities.* Lanham, MD: American Correctional Association.

Ashman, A. 1982. Prisoners. . . Overnight Visitation. *ABA Journal.* July.

Association on Programs for Female Offenders. 1981. *Survey of Correctional Administrators.* Jessup, MD: Maryland Correctional Institution for Women.

Balasco-Barr, P. 1995. Commentary: Breaking the Cycle of Crime. *Corrections Today.* December.

Barry, E. with R. Ginchild and D. Lee. 1995. Legal Issues for Prisoners with Children. In Gabel and Johnston, eds. *Children of Incarcerated Parents.* New York: Lexington Books.

Bates, T. M. 1989. Rethinking Conjugal Visitation in Light of the 'AIDS' Crisis. *New England Journal on Criminal and Civil Confinement.* Winter.

Baunach, P. J. 1979. The Separation of Inmate-Mothers from Their Children. Manuscript draft, Washington, D.C. September.

___.1982. You Can't Be a Mother and Be in Prison. . . Can You? Impacts of the Mother-Child Separation. In *The Criminal Justice System and Women,* B. R. Price and N. J. Sokoloff, eds. New York: Clark Boardman Company, Ltd.

___. 1984. *Mothers in Prison.* New Brunswick, NJ: Rutgers/Transaction Books.

Bayse, Daniel J. 1991. *As Free As An Eagle—The Inmate's Family Survival Guide.* Laurel, MD: American Correctional Association.

___. 1993. *Helping Hands—A Handbook for Volunteers in Prisons and Jails.* Laurel, MD: American Correctional Association.

Beavers-Luteran, B. A. 1971. Mother/Child Retreats. *Corrections Today.* 33.

Becker, B .L. 1991. Order in the Court: Challenging Judges Who Incarcerate Pregnant, Substance-Dependent Defendants to Protect Fetal Health. *Hastings Constitutional Law Quarterly* 19(1).

Beckerman, Adela. 1994. Mothers in Prison: Meeting the Prerequisite Conditions for Permanency Planning. *Social Work* 39 (1), January.

Bish, M., L. Denton, and L. Gonzalez. 1993. Intervention Strategies for Families of Offenders: The Pyramid Model. In *Proceedings of the Fourth North American Conference on Family and Corrections.* 1993. Quebec City, Quebec, Canada (October 10-12). Available from the National Institute of Corrections Information Center.

Blakeley, S. 1995. California Program to Focus on New Mothers. *Corrections Today.* December.

Bloom, B. 1995. Public Policy and the *Children of Incarcerated Parents.* In K. Gabel and D. Johnston, eds. *Children of Incarcerated Parents.* New York: Lexington Books.

Bornstein, M. H., ed. *Handbook of Parenting: Vol. 4. Applied and Practical Parenting, Part 1: Applied Issues in Parenting.* Hillsdale, NJ: Erlbaum.

Boudouris, J. 1971. Homicide and the Family. *Journal of Marriage and the Family.* November.

___. 1976. The Politics of Research. In Riedel and Chappell, eds. *Issues in Criminal Justice: Planning and Evaluation.* New York: Praeger Publishers.

___. 1984. Recidivism as a Process. *Journal of Offender Counseling, Services & Rehabilitation* . 8(3).

___. 1985. *Prisons and Kids.* College Park, MD: American Correctional Association.

REFERENCES

___. 1988. The Politics of Research Revisited. *Journal of Offender Counseling, Services & Rehabilitation* 13(1).

Bowlby, J. 1951. *Maternal Care and Mental Health*. New York: Schocken Books.

Bradshaw, John. 1995. *Family Secrets: What You Don't Know Can Hurt You*. New York: Bantam.

Breen, P. A. 1995a. Advocacy Efforts on Behalf of the *Children of Incarcerated Parents*. In K. Gabel and D. Johnston, eds. *Children of Incarcerated Parents*. New York: Lexington Books.

___. 1995b. Bridging the Barriers. *Corrections Today*. December.

Brodie, D. L. 1982. Babies Behind Bars: Should Incarcerated Mothers Be Allowed to Keep Their Newborns with Them in Prison? *University of Richmond Law Review*. 16.

Brody, J .E. 1983. Influential Theory on 'Bonding' at Birth is Now Questioned. *New York Times* March 29.

Bronfenbrenner, U. and P. R. Neville. 1994. America's Children and Families: An International Perspective. In S. L. Kagan and B. Weissbourd, eds. *Putting Families First: America's Family Support Movement and the Challenge of Change*. San Francisco: Jossey-Bass.

Bruch, H. 1952. *Don't Be Afraid of Your Child*. New York: Farrar, Straus and Young.

Buckles, D. A., and M. A. LaFazia. 1973. Child Care for Mothers in Prison. In *Social Work Practice and Social Justice*. B. Ross and C. Shireman, eds. New York: National Association of Social Workers.

Burke, M. 1981. Mexico's New Prisons. *Corrections Today*. 42.

Burton-Barnett, C. and C. Cameron. 1993. Project SEEK (Services to Enable and Empower Kids). In *Proceedings of the Fourth North American Conference on Family and Corrections*. 1993. Quebec City, Quebec, Canada (October 10-12). Available from the National Institute of Corrections Information Center.

Canadian Family Hospitality Homes. 1993. In *Proceedings of the Fourth North American Conference on Family and Corrections*. 1993. Quebec City, Quebec, Canada (October 10-12). Available from the National Institute of Corrections Information Center.

Cannings, K. L. 1990. *Bridging the Gap: Programs and Services Facilitate Contact Between Inmate Parents and their Children*. Corrections Branch, Secretariat, Ministry of the Solicitor General of Canada.

Carlson, B. E., and N. Cervera. 1991. Inmates and Their Families: Conjugal Visits, Family Contact, and Family Functioning. *Criminal Justice and Behavior*. September.

Catan, L. 1992. Infants with Mothers in Prison. In Shaw, R., ed., *Prisoners' Children: What Are the Issues?* New York: Routledge.

Cavan, R., and E. S. Zemans. 1958. Marital Relationships of Prisoners in 28 Countries. *Journal of Criminal Law, Criminology, and Police Science* 49.

Chaiklin, H. 1972. Integrating Correctional and Family Systems. *American Journal of Orthopsychiatry* 42.

Chaneles, S. 1973. *The Open Prison: Saving Their Lives and Our Money*. New York: The Dial Press.

Chesney-Lind, M., and R. Immarigeon. 1995. "Alternatives to Women's Incarceration." In K. Gabel and D. Johnston, eds. *Children of Incarcerated Parents*. New York: Lexington Books.

Chess, S., and A. Thomas. 1982. Infant Bonding: Mystique and Reality. *American Journal of Orthopsychiatry*. 52.

Christie, N. 1994. *Crime Control as Industry: Towards GULAGS, Western Style. 2d. ed.* New York: Routledge.

Clark, Cheryl L. Sisters Are Doing it Themselves. In *Juvenile and Adult Boot Camps*. 1996. Lanham, Maryland: American Correctional Association.

Clement, M. J. 1993. Parenting in Prison: A National Survey of Programs for Incarcerated Women. *Journal of Offender Rehabilitation*. 19.

CorrectCare. 1995. California Study Examines TB, HIV, and Hepatitis. December.

Couturier, Lance. 1995. Inmates Benefit from Family Services Programs. *Corrections Today*. December.

Criminal Justice Newsletter. 1991. Court Upholds Alabama Policy of Segregating Inmates with HIV. October 1.

REFERENCES

Daly, K., S. Geballe, and S. Wheeler. 1988. Litigation-Driven Research: A Case Study of Lawyer/Social Scientist Collaboration. *Women's Rights Law Reporter*. Fall.

Deck, M.V. 1988. Incarcerated Mothers and Their Infants: Separation or Legislation? *Boston College Law Review*. May.

Dobyns, L., and C. Crawford-Mason. 1994. *Thinking About Quality: Progress, Wisdom, and the Deming Philosophy*. New York: Random House.

Douglas, M. C. 1993. The Mutter-Kind-Heim at Frankfurt am Main: 'Come Together - Go Together'. An Observation. *International Journal of Comparative and Applied Criminal Justice*. Spring.

Driscoll, D. 1985. Mother's Day Once a Month. *Corrections Today*. August.

Einsele, H., and B. Maelicke. 1980. *Anlaufstelle Fur Straffallig Gewordene Frauen: Endbericht der Wissenschaftlichen Begleitung*. Rand 90, Schriftenreihe des Bundesministers fur Jugend, Familie and Gesundheit. Stuttgart: Verlag W. Kohlhammer.

Family & Corrections Network Report. 1994. Children of Incarcerated Parents. December.

___. 1995. Parenting Programs for Prisoners. June.

Federal Republic of Germany. *Justizvollzugsplan fur das Land Schleswig-Holstein*. Schriftenreihe der Landesregierung Schleswig-Holstein, undated.

___. *Strafvollzug in Bayern*. Bayerisches Staatsministerium der Justiz, undated.

___. *Mutter-Kind-Heim in der Frauenvollzugsanstalt Frankfurt am Main-Preungesheim*. Kinderheim Preungesheim e. V., undated.

___. 1978. "Nr. 117. Richtlinien Fur das Mutter-Kind-Heim der Justizvollzugsanstalt." *Justiz-Ministerial-Blatt Fur Hessen* 30. Wiesbaden. October 15.

___. 1982. *Frauenkriminalitat und Frauenstrafvollzug in Nordrhein-Westfalen*. Dusseldorf: Nordrhein-Westfalen Justizminister.

Feeley, M. M. 1991. The Privatization of Prisons in Historical Perspective. *Criminal Justice Research* Bulletin. 6/2.

Fingarette, H. 1988. *Heavy Drinking—The Myth of Alcoholism as a Disease*. Berkeley, CA: University of California Press.

Fishman, S. H. and A. S. Alissi. 1979. Strengthening Families as Natural Support Systems for Offenders. *Federal Probation*. 43.

Fuller, L. G. 1993. Visitors to Women's Prisons in California: An Exploratory Study. *Federal Probation*. December.

Gabel, K., and D. Johnston, eds. 1995. *Children of Incarcerated Parents*. New York: Lexington Books.

Gabel, K., and Girard, K. 1995. Long-Term Care Nurseries in Prisons: A Descriptive Study. In K. Gabel and D. Johnston, eds. *Children of Incarcerated Parents*. New York: Lexington Books.

Gaudin, J. M., Jr. 1984. Social Work Roles and Tasks With Incarcerated Mothers. *Social Casework*. May.

Genty, P. M. 1995. Termination of Parental Rights Among Prisoners—A National Perspective. In K. Gabel and D. Johnston, eds. *Children of Incarcerated Parents*. New York: Lexington Books.

Gil, D. G. 1971. Violence Against Children. *Journal of Marriage and the Family*. November.

Glasser, I. 1990. Maintaining the Bond: Niantic Parenting Programs. Parenting Grant #90CW0926, Washington, D.C.: United States Department of Health and Human Services, Office of Human Development Services, Administration for Children, Youth, and Families.

___. 1993. Mothers in Prison in World Perspective. In *Proceedings of the Fourth North American Conference on Family and Corrections*. 1993. Quebec City, Quebec, Canada (October 10-12). Available from the National Institute of Corrections Information Center.

Goetting, A. 1982a. Conjugal Association in Prison: Issues and Perspectives. *Crime and Delinquency*. 28.

___. 1982b. Conjugal Association in Prison: A World View. *Criminal Justice Abstracts*. 14.

___. Commentary: Conjugal Association in Prison: The Debate and Its Resolution. *New England Journal on Prison Law*. 8.

REFERENCES

___. 1984. Conjugal Association Practices in Prisons of the American Nations. *Alternative Lifestyles*. 6.

Goode, W. J. 1971. Force and Violence in the Family. *Journal of Marriage and the Family*. November.

Greening, B. 1978. A Prison for Moms and Kids. *California Youth Authority Quarterly. 31*

Hairston, C. F. 1992. Family Ties During Imprisonment: Important to Whom and for What? *The Prison Journal*. Spring and *Journal of Sociology and Social Welfare*. Undated.

___. 1995. Fathers in Prison. In K. Gabel and D. Johnston, eds. *Children of Incarcerated Parents*. New York: Lexington Books.

Hairston, C. F., and P. M. Hess. 1989. Family Ties: Maintaining Child-Parent Bonds Is Important. *Corrections Today*. April.

Hairston, C. F., and P. W. Lockett. 1985. Parents in Prison: A Child Abuse and Neglect Prevention Strategy. *Child Abuse and Neglect*. 9.

___. 1987. Parents in Prison: New Directions for Social Services. *Social Work*. 323(2).

Haley, K. 1977. Mothers Behind Bars: A Look at the Parental Rights of Incarcerated Women. *New England Journal on Prison Law*. 4.

Harris, J. W. 1993. Comparison of Stressors Among Female vs. Male Inmates. *Journal of Offender Rehabilitation*. 19:1/2.

Harris, Z. 1996. How to Help the Children When Mothers Go to Jail. *American Jails* January/February.

Henriques, Z. W. 1982. *Imprisoned Mothers and Their Children*. Washington, D.C.: University Press of America, Inc.

Herman, M. G., and M. G. Haft, eds. 1973. *Prisoners' Rights Sourcebook*. New York: Clark Boardman Co., Ltd.

Hoffman, S. L. 1977. What Happens When a Mother Goes to Prison? An Overview of Relevant Legal and Psychological Considerations. Paper presented at the meeting of the American Psychology-Law Society.

Holt, N., and D. Miller. 1972. *Explorations in Inmate-Family Relationships*. Sacramento, CA: California Department of Corrections.

Holt, K. E. 1981-1982. Nine Months to Life—The Law and the Pregnant Inmate. *Journal of Family Law* 29.

Hungerford, G. P. 1993. Executive Summary: The Children of Inmate Mothers in Ohio. Columbus, Ohio: Center for Peace Studies and Community Development, Inc. and Columbus Foundation.

Immarigeon, R. 1994. When Parents Are Sent to Prison. *National Prison Project Journal*. Fall.

Jamison, J. D. 1984. Massachusetts Correctional Institution—Framingham Parenting Programs. Unpublished manuscript.

Janes, R. W. 1993. Total Quality Management: Can It Work in Federal Probation? *Federal Probation*. December.

Johnson, E. H. 1990. Open Prisons in the Japanese Manner. *International Journal of Comparative and Applied Criminal Justice*. Spring.

Johnston, D. 1995. Parent-Child Visitation in the Jail or Prison. In Gabel and Johnston, eds., *Children of Incarcerated Parents*. New York: Lexington Books.

Johnston, D., and K. Gabel. 1995. Incarcerated Parents. In K. Gabel and D. Johnston, eds. *Children of Incarcerated Parents*. New York: Lexington Books.

Jose-Kampfner, Christina. 1991. Michigan Program Makes Children's Visits Meaningful. *Corrections Today*. August.

Kagan, S. L. and B. Weissbourd, eds. 1994. *Putting Families First: America's Family Support Movement and the Challenge of Change*. San Francisco: Jossey-Bass.

___. 1994a. Toward a New Normative System of Family Support. In S. L. Kagan and B. Weissbourd, eds. *Putting Families First.: America's Family Support Movement and the Challenge of Change*. San Francisco: Jossey-Bass.

Key, D. 1993. Someone to Come Home To: Parenting Programs for Men in Prison. In *Proceedings of the Fourth North American Conference on Family and Corrections*. 1993. Quebec City, Quebec, Canada (October 10-12). Available from the National Institute of Corrections Information Center.

REFERENCES

Kimbrell, V. 1994. Mothers in Prison: Safeguarding the Parent-Child Relationship. *Clearinghouse Review*. July.

Klaus, M. I., and J. H. Kennell. 1976. *Maternal-Infant Bonding: The Impact of Early Separation or Loss on Family Development*. St. Louis, Missouri: C.V. Mosby.

Koban, L. A. 1983. Parents in Prison: A Comparative Analysis of the Effects of Incarceration on the Families of Men and Women. *Research in Law, Deviance and Social Control*. 5.

Lamb, M. 1982. Second Thoughts on First Touch. *Psychology Today*. 16.

Lanier, C. S., Jr. 1991. Dimensions of Father-Child Interaction in a New York State Prison Population. *Journal of Offender Rehabilitation*. 16:3/4.

LeFlore, L. and M. A. Holston. 1989. Perceived Importance of Parenting Behaviors as Reported by Inmate Mothers: an Exploratory Study. *Journal of Offender Counseling, Services and Rehabilitation*. 14.

Lloyd, E. 1992. Prisoners' Children: the Role of Prison Visitors' Centres. In Shaw, R., ed. *Prisoners' Children: What Are the Issues*? New York: Routledge.

Logan, C. 1990. *Private Prisons, Cons and Pros*. New York: Oxford University Press.

Marcus, S. E. 1995. Child Welfare System Policies and the *Children of Incarcerated Parents*. In K. Gabel and D. Johnston, eds. *Children of Incarcerated Parents*. New York: Lexington Books.

Martin, S. L., and N. U. Cotten. 1995. Literacy Intervention for Incarcerated Women: the Motheread Program. *Corrections Today*. December.

McCarthy, B. R. 1979. Experiences of Female Inmates on Temporary Release From Incarceration. In *Proceedings of the Southern Conference on Corrections*, edited by V. Fox. Tallahassee, FL: Florida State University.

___. 1980. Inmate Mothers: The Problems of Separation and Reintegration. *Journal of Offender Counseling, Services and Rehabilitation*. 4.

McGowan, B. G., and K. L. Blumenthal. 1978. *Why Punish the Children? A Study of Children of Women Prisoners*. Hackensack, NJ: National Council on Crime and Delinquency.

McHugh, G. A. 1980. Protection of the Rights of Pregnant Women in Prisons and Detention Facilities. *New England Journal on Prison Law*. 6.

Mead, M. 1954. Some Theoretical Considerations on the Problem of Mother-Child Separation. *American Journal of Orthopsychiatry*. 24.

Metzler, D. K. 1994. Neglected by the System: Children of Incarcerated Mothers. *Illinois Bar Journal*. August.

Morin, L. 1993. Clinique Societe Emmanuel-Gregoire. In *Proceedings of the Fourth North American Conference on Family and Corrections*. 1993. Quebec City, Quebec, Canada (October 10-12). Available from the National Institute of Corrections Information Center.

Moses, Marilyn C. 1993. Girl Scouts Behind Bars: New Program at Women's Prison Benefits Mothers and Children. *Corrections Today*. August.

___. 1995. A Synergistic Solution for Children of Incarcerated Parents: Girl Scouts Beyond Bars. *Corrections Today*. December.

Murton, T. 1983a. The Penal Colony: Relic or Reform? Paper presented at meeting of the Western Society of Criminology.

___. 1983b. Penal Slavery, Flogging, Community-Based Corrections, and Other Reforms. Paper presented at criminal justice conference, Des Moines, Iowa.

Mustin, J. W. 1991. The Family: A Critical Factor for Corrections. *Nurturing Today*. X (1).

National Commission on Correctional Health Care. 1994. Position Statement. Administrative Management of HIV in Corrections. September 25.

National Law Journal. 1989. Case of the Week—Two Incarcerated Fathers Lose Rights. August 14.

REFERENCES

Neto, V. V., and L. M. Bainer. 1982. *Mother and Wife Locked Up: A Day With the Family.* San Rafael, CA: Social Action Research Center.

Newsweek. 1976. Nurseries in the Jailhouse. January 12.

Norman, J. 1995. Children of Prisoners in Foster Care. In K. Gabel and D. Johnston, eds. *Children of Incarcerated Parents.* New York: Lexington Books.

Palmer, R. 1972. The Prisoner-Mother and Her Child. *Capital University Law Review*. 1.

Poe, L. 1995. A Program for Grandparent Caregivers. In K. Gabel and D. Johnston, eds. *Children of Incarcerated Parents*. New York: Lexington Books.

Powell, D. R. 1994. Evaluating Family Support Programs: Are We Making Progress? In S. L. Kagan and B. Weissbourd, eds. *Putting Families First: America's Family Support Movement and the Challenge of Change*. San Francisco: Jossey-Bass.

Proceedings of the Fourth North American Conference on the Family and Corrections. 1993. Exploring the Family Side of Justice. Quebec City, Quebec, Canada. October 10-12. Available from the National Institute of Corrections Information Center.

Richards, M. 1992. The Separation of Children and Parents. In Shaw, R., ed., *Prisoners' Children: What Are the Issues*? New York: Routledge.

Riedel, M., and D. Chappell, eds. 1976. *Issues in Criminal Justice: Planning and Evaluation*. New York: Praeger Publishers.

Rosenkrantz, L., and V. Joshua. 1982. Children of Incarcerated Parents: A Hidden Population. *Children Today.* 11.

Roulet, Sister E., P. O'Rourke, and M. Reichers. 1993. The Children's Center - Bedford Hills Correctional Facility. In *Proceedings of the Fourth North American Conference on Family and Corrections.* 1993. Quebec City, Quebec, Canada (October 10-12). Available from the National Institute of Corrections Information Center.

Rutter, M. 1971. Parent-Child Separation: Psychological Effects on the Children. *Journal of Child Psychology and Psychiatry.*12.

___. 1979. Maternal Deprivation, 1972-1978: New Findings, New Concepts, New Approaches. *Child Development.* 50.

___. 1995a. Maternal Deprivation. In Bornstein, ed, *Handbook of Parenting*. Hillside, NJ: Erlbaum.

___. 1995b. Clinical Implications of Attachment Concepts: Retrospect and Prospect. *Journal of Child Psychology and Psychiatry.* 36.

Sack, W. H. 1977. Children of Imprisoned Fathers. *Psychiatry*. 40.

Sack, W. H., Seidler, J., and S. Thomas. 1976. The Children of Imprisoned Parents: A Psychosocial Exploration. *American Journal of Orthopsychiatry*. 46.

Sack, W. H. and J. Seidler. 1978. Should Children Visit Their Parents in Prison? *Law and Human Behavior.* 2(3).

Samenow, S. E. 1984. *Inside the Criminal Mind*. New York: Times Books.

Sametz, L. 1980. Children of Incarcerated Women. *Social Work.* 25.

Saylor, W. G. and E. B. Gilman. 1995. Modelling and Graphing Organizational Processes to Establish and Maintain Performance Benchmarks: Methods for the Systematic Application, Evaluation and Evolution of Performance Measures. Paper prepared for The Academy of Criminal Justice Sciences Meeting in Boston. March 8.

Selber, K., T. Johnson, and M. Lauderdale. 1993. The FSP/Community Support Model: Natural Support Networks. In *Proceedings of the Fourth North American Conference on Family and Corrections.* 1993. Quebec City, Quebec, Canada (October 10-12). Available from the National Institute of Corrections Information Center.

Shaw, M. 1992. Issues of Power and Control: Women in Prison and Their Defenders. *British Journal of Criminology*. Autumn.

Shaw, R. 1987. *Children of Imprisoned Fathers*. London: Hodder & Stoughton.

___, ed. 1992a. *Prisoners' Children: What Are the Issues?* New York: Routledge

REFERENCES

___. 1992b. Imprisoned Fathers and the Orphans of Justice. In Shaw, R., ed. *Prisoners' Children: What Are the Issues?* New York: Routledge

___. 1992c. Conclusion: Politics, Policy, and Practice. In Shaw, R., ed. *Prisoners' Children: What Are the Issues?* New York: Routledge.

Showalter, D., and W. W. Jones. 1980. Marital and Family Counseling in Prisons. *Social Work*. 25.

Simbro, W. 1995. Many Children of Prisoners Not Forgotten. *Des Moines Register*. December. 23.

Slagle, T. 1981. Childrearing Attitudes of Incarcerated Women. Unpublished manuscript. University of Maryland Institute for Child Study.

Smith, G. 1995. Practical Considerations Regarding Termination of Incarcerated Parents' Rights. In K. Gabel and D. Johnston, eds. *Children of Incarcerated Parents*. New York: Lexington Books.

Stanton, A.M. 1980. *When Mothers Go To Jail*. Lexington, MA: Lexington Books.

Star, D. 1981. Community Treatment Programs for Inmate-Mothers and Their Infants: An Evaluation of the 1980 Implementation of Assembly Bill 512. Unpublished report to the California Legislature.

Stumbo, N. J., and S. L. Little. 1990. Camp Celebration: Incarcerated Mothers and Their Children Camping Together. United States Department of Health and Human Services Grant No. 90CW0927 and National Institute of Corrections.

___. 1991. Campground Offers Relaxed Setting for Children's Visitation Program. *Corrections Today* August.

Taylor, H. L., and B. M. Durr. 1977. Preschool in Prison. *Young Children*. 32.

Trabut, C. 1993. Reflections on the Acceptance Given in a Penitentiary Setting to Children Left in the Care of their Incarcerated Mothers. In *Proceedings of the Fourth North American Conference of Family and Corrections*. 1993. Quebec City, Quebec, Canada (October 10-12). Available from the National Institute of Corrections Information Center.

Trepanier, Y. 1993. (C.F.A.D.) Continuite-Famille Aupres des Detenues. In *Proceedings of the Fourth North American Conference of Family and Corrections*. 1993. Quebec City, Quebec, Canada (October 10-12). Available from the National Institute of Corrections Information Center.

United States Department of Health and Human Services, National Institutes of Health, National Institute of Child Health and Human Development. 1996. Infant Child Care and Attachment Security: Results of the NICHD Study of Early Child Care. *News Notes* and Report presented at the International Conference on Infant Studies, Providence, R.I. April 20.

United States Department of Justice, Bureau of Justice Statistics. 1986. Prisoners in 1985. June.

___. 1987. Correctional Populations in the United States 1985. December.

___. 1995a. Prisoners in 1994. August.

___.1995b. HIV in Prisons and Jails, 1993. August.

___. 1995c. Correctional Populations in the United States, 1993. October.

___. 1995d. State and Federal Prisons Report Record Growth During Last 12 Months." Press Release. December 3.

___. 1996. HIV in Prisons 1994. March.

United States Department of Justice, Federal Bureau of Prisons. 1995. Parenting Program Standards—PS/5355.03. January 20.

United States Department of Justice, Law Enforcement Assistance Administration. 1979. *Uniform Law Commissioners' Model Sentencing and Corrections Act*.

United States Department of Justice, National Institute of Justice. 1995. 1994 Update: HIV/AIDS and STDs in Correctional Facilities. December. Prepared by Abt Associates, Inc. for the National Institute of Justice and the Centers for Disease Control and Prevention.

Walker, N. 1992. Introduction: Theory, Practice, and an Example. In Shaw, R., ed. *Prisoners' Children: What Are the Issues?* New York: Routledge.

REFERENCES

Walton, M. 1986. *The Deming Management Method.* New York: Putnam Publishing Group.

Weilerstein, R. 1995. The Prison MATCH Program. In K. Gabel and D. Johnston, eds. *Children of Incarcerated Parents.* New York: Lexington Books.

Weissbourd, B. 1994. The Evolution of the Family Support Movement. In S. L. Kagan and B. Weissbourd, eds. *Putting Families First: America's Family Support Movement and the Challenge of Change.* San Francisco: Jossey-Bass.

Wilkinson, W. V. 1990. An Exploration of the Mexican Criminal Justice System: Interviews with Incarcerated Inmates in a Mexican Prison. *International Journal of Comparative and Applied Criminal Justice.* Spring.

Woodrow, J. 1992. Mothers Inside, Children Outside. In Shaw, R., ed. *Prisoners' Children: What Are the Issues?* New York: Routledge.

Wooldredge, J. D. and K. Masters. 1993. Confronting Problems Faced by Pregnant Inmates in State Prisons. *Crime and Delinquency*. April.

Yale Law Journal. 1978. On Prisoners and Parenting: Preserving the Tie That Binds. 87.

Yochelson, S. and S. E. Samenow. 1975. *The Criminal Personality. Volume II: The Change Process.* New York: Jason Aronson.

Zambrowsky, J. 1984. Limited Access Correctional Communities or Penal Colonies. *Liaison* 10. Monthly publication of the Canadian Ministry of the Solicitor General.

Ziegler, E. F. 1994. Foreword. In S. L. Kagan and B. Weissbourd, eds. *Putting Families First: America's Family Support Movement and the Challenge of Change*. San Francisco: Jossey-Bass.

8. Resources

Contacts

Alabama

Shirlie Lobmiller, Warden
Julia Tutwiler Prison for Women
Route 1, Box 33
Wetumpka 36092-9199
(205) 567-4369
FAX: (205) 567-4369 (x234)

Reneice Bellamy, Director, AIM, Inc.
Julia Tutwiler Prison for Women
Box 986
Montgomery 36101-0986
(800) 679-0246

Alaska

Mike Wehrer, Superintendent
Meadow Creek Correctional Center
P.O. Box 600
Eagle River 99577
(907) 694-9511

Frank Sauser, Director
Division of Institutions
4500 Diplomacy Dr., Suite 207
Anchorage 99508-5918
(907) 269-7405

Arizona

Phil Jungers, CPS
Arizona State Prison Complex
Phoenix
342 N. 32nd Street
Box 52109
Phoenix 85072
(602) 255-3132
FAX: (602)255-2244

Gail Hamilton, Program Manager
Arizona State Prison Complex
Perryville
P.O. Box 3000
Goodyear 85338
(602) 853-0304 (x4111)

Arkansas

Virginia Wallace, Warden
Tucker Unit for Women
2400 State Farm Road
P.O. Box 240
Tucker 72168-0240
(501) 842-2519

California

Sharrell Blakeley, Assistant Director (Phone: 916-445-5147)
Marc Stambuk, Correctional Counselor (Phone: 916-445-5146)
Office of Community Resources and Development
California Department of Corrections
P.O. Box 942883
Sacramento 94283-0001
(916) 445-5147

Susan Poole, Warden
California Institution for Women
P.O. Box 6000
Corona 91718
(909) 597-1771
FAX: (909) 393-8061

Teena Farmon, Warden (Phone: 209-665-5351)
D. L. Ollison (Phone: 209-665-5515)
Central California Women's Facility
23370 Road 22
P.O. Box 1501
Chowchilla 93610-1501
(209) 665-5531
FAX: (209) 665-7158

Mamie S. Lockette, Warden
Lt. Darren Bobella
Northern California Women's Facility
P.O. Box 213006
Stockton 952139006
(209) 943-1600
FAX: (209) 463-5382

Lew Kuykendall, Warden
Valley State Prison for Women
21633 Avenue 24
P.O. Box 99
Chowchilla 93610-0099
(209) 665-6100
FAX: (209) 665-6102
FAX: (209) 833-7599

Jean E. Anderson, Warden
California Rehabilitation Center
5th Street and Western
P.O. Box 1841
Norco 91760
(909) 737-2683
FAX: (909) 736-1488

Frank Powell, Warden
Sierra Conservation Center
5100 O'Byrnes Ferry Road
P.O. Box 497
Jamestown 95327
(209) 984-5291
FAX: (209) 984-3607

Colorado

Mike Williams, Superintendent
Colorado Women's Correctional Facility
P.O. Box 500
Canon City 81215
(719) 269-4715

Connecticut

Carol A. Dunn, Warden
Mary A. Gibson, Parent Child Counselor
Connecticut Correctional Institution
Niantic
199 W. Main Street
Niantic 06357
(860) 691-6529

Delaware

Anita Davenport, Program Director
Delores J. Baylor Women's Correctional Institution
660 Baylor Boulevard
New Castle 19720
(302) 577-3004 (x1104)

Paul Howard, Warden
Women's Correctional Institution
100 Darley Road
Claymont 19703
(302) 571-3004

District of Columbia

Jim Reddick, Deputy Warden
Correctional Treatment Facility
1901 E. St. S.E.
Washington 20003
(202) 673-8046

Florida

Dr. William Bales
Chief, Bureau of Planning, Research and Statistics
Florida Department of Corrections
2601 Blair Stone Road
Tallahassee 32399-2500
(904) 488-1801

John Dale, Superintendent
Sherry D. Waters, Classifications Supervisor
Jefferson Correctional Institution
Drawer 430
Monticello 323440430
(904) 997-1987
FAX: (904) 997-0791

H. Hayes, Assistant Superintendent
Florida Correctional Institution
P.O. Box 147
Lowell 32663-0147
(352) 622-5151

Beverleena Jeter-Brown, Superintendent
Robin R. Pendleton, Assistant Superintendent
Broward Correctional Institution
P.O. Box 8540
Pembroke Pines 33024
(954) 434-0050
FAX: (954) 434-7800

Georgia

Mary Esposito, Warden
Fran Standifer, Project REACH Director
(Phone: 404-624-2200)
Metro Women's Correctional Institution
1301 Constitution Road, S.E.
Atlanta 30316
(404) 624-1411
FAX: (404) 624-7419

Hawaii

Jo desMaretes, Offender Services Administrator
Women's Community Correctional Center
42477 Kalanianole Highway
Kailua 96734
(808) 266-9662

Idaho

Bona Miller, Warden
Angela Blom, Public Information Officer
Pocatello Women's Correctional Center
1451 Fore Road
P.O. Box 6049
Pocatello 83205
(208) 236-6360
FAX: (208) 236-6362

Illinois
Gwendolyn V. Thornton, Warden
Jeanne Fairman, Family Services Supervisor
Dwight Correctional Center
P.O. Box 5001
Dwight 60420-5001
(815) 584-2806
FAX: (815) 584-2889

Indiana
Dana L. Blank, Superintendent
Deborah Sutton, Program Coordinator
Indiana Women's Prison
401 N. Randolph Street
Indianapolis 46201
(317) 639-2671

Iowa
Glenna Munson, Director
Peggy Blazek, Manager
Women's Residential Correctional Facility
1917 Hickman
Des Moines 50314
(515) 242-6320
FAX: (515) 242-6328

Sally Chandler Halford, Director
Iowa Department of Corrections
Capitol Annex
Des Moines 50319
(515) 281-4360

Barbara Olk Long, Warden
Iowa Correctional Institution for Women
Mitchellville 50169
(515) 967-4236
FAX: (515) 967-5347

Kansas
Leo Taylor, Warden
Susan Cavanaugh, Coordinator
Topeka Correctional Facility
815 S.E. Rice Road
Topeka 66607
(913) 296-7220
FAX: (913) 296-0184

Kentucky
Betty Kassulke, Warden
David Buckman, Psychologist
Kentucky Correctional Institution for Women
Ash Avenue
Box 337
Pewee Valley 40056
(502) 241-8454
FAX: (502) 241-0372

Louisiana
Nellie Fanguy, Deputy Warden
Louisiana Correctional Institute for Women
P.O. Box 26
St. Gabriel 70776
(504) 642-5529
FAX: (504) 642-7757

Maine
James Clemons, Superintendent
Maine Correctional Center
17 Mallison Falls Road
Windham 04082-1197
(207) 892-6716
FAX: (207) 892-0663

Maryland
Thomas R. Corcoran, Warden
Maryland Correctional PreRelease System
P.O. Box 537
Jessup 20794
(410) 799-1363
FAX: (410) 799-9479

Barbara Shaw, Administrator
Patricia Allen
(Phone 410-799-1363)
Baltimore PreRelease Unit for Women
301 N. Calverton Road
Baltimore 21223
(410) 566-5747
FAX: (410) 947-1064

Joseph Henneberry, Director
Kathleen Flanagan, Facility Coordinator
Patuxent Institution for Women
Jessup
(410) 799-3400

Massachusetts
Katherine A. Chmiel, Superintendent
Jane D. Jamison, Parenting Coordinator
Massachusetts Correctional Institution
P.O. Box 9007
Framingham 01701-9007
(617) 727-5056
FAX: (617) 727-0527

Luis Spencer, Superintendent
Martin Shaughnessy
Lancaster PreRelease Center
P.O. Box 123
Lancaster 01523
(617) 727-8016

Michigan

Robin Cooley, Program Director
Camp Branch
19 Fourth Street
Coldwater 49036
(517) 278-3204 (x310)

Joan N. Yukins, Warden
Scott Correctional Facility
47500 Five Mile Road
Plymouth 48170
(313) 459-7400

Minnesota

Connie Roehrich, Warden
Dianne Hagen, Parenting Coordinator
Phone (612) 496-4480
Minnesota Correctional Facility Shakopee
1010 W. 6th Ave.
Shakopee 55379
(612) 496-4440
FAX: (612) 496-4476

Mississippi

Lora H. Cole, Warden
Central Mississippi Correctional Facility
P.O. Box 88550
Pearl 39208
(601) 932-2880

Missouri

Bryan Goeke, Superintendent
June Pearce, PATCH Program
Renz Correctional Center
P.O. Box 3200
Jefferson City 65102
(314) 751-4748
FAX: (314) 751-4403

Montana

Anne Ross, Clinical Programs Coordinator
Women's Correctional Center
Drawer C
Warm Springs 59756-0217
(406) 247-5111

Nebraska

Lawrence L. Wayne, Warden
Mary Alley, Coordinator, Project M.O.L.D.
Renee Uldrich, Nursery Instructor
Nebraska Center for Women
Route 1
Box 33
York 68467-9714
(402) 362-3317
FAX: (402) 362-3317

Nevada

Miles Long, Warden
Janice Bengler Phone (702) 887-3472
Nevada Women's Correctional Center
P.O. Box 7007
Carson City 89702
(702) 887-3475

Lt. Cheri McKee, Manager
B. Cordova, Caseworker
Silver Springs Conservation Camp
P.O. Box 810
Silver Springs 89429-0810
(702) 577-2662

New Hampshire

Jane Coplan, Superintendent
New Hampshire State Prison for Women
317 Mast Road
Goffstown 03045
(603) 668-6137

New Jersey

Charlotte Blackwell, Superintendent
Helen Adams, Director of Social Services
Edna Mahan Correctional Facility for Women
Drawer E
Clinton 08809
(908) 735-7111

New Mexico

Tom Newton, Warden
Penny Lucero, Assistant Warden
New Mexico Women's Correctional Facility
1700 East Old Highway 66
P.O. Box 800
Grants 87020
(505) 287-2941
FAX: (505) 285-6828

New York

Elaine Lord, Superintendent
Joseph T. Smith, Deputy Superintendent
Sister Elaine Roulet, Director of Children's Center
Patricia O'Rourke, Assistant Director, Children's Center
Bedford Hills Correctional Facility
247 Harris Road
Bedford Hills 10507-2496
(914) 241-3100

Bridget Gladwin, Superintendent
Jose Morales, Deputy Superintendent, Program Services
Taconic Correctional Facility
250 Harris Road
Bedford Hills 10507-2498
(914) 241-3010

North Carolina

Carol Caldwell, Superintendent
Pat Vincitorio, Social Work Supervisor
Correctional Institution for Women
1034 Bragg Street
Raleigh 27610
(919) 733-4340

Janet Bullock, Superintendent
Fountain Correctional Center for Women
P.O. Box 1435
Rocky Mount 27802
(919) 442-9712

Laura B. Overstreet, Superintendent
Wilmington Residential Facility for Women
P.O. Box 5354
Wilmington 28403-4155
(910) 251-2671

North Dakota

Don Redmann, Accreditation Director
North Dakota State Penitentiary
P.O. Box 5521
Bismarck 58502-5521
(701) 328-6114
FAX: (701) 328-6640

Ohio

Christine Money, Warden
Sandy Goodwin, Correctional Program Coordinator
Ohio Reformatory for Women
1479 Collins Ave.
Marysville 43040
(513) 642-1065
FAX: (513) 644-8172

Dr. Barbara Brown Nichols, Warden
Bud Sellars, Administrative Assistant
Franklin PreRelease Center
1800 Harmon Ave.
P.O. Box 23651
Columbus 43223
(614) 445-8600
FAX: (614) 444-8267

Oklahoma

Neville Massie, Warden
Rita Cooksey, Case Manager Coordinator
Mabel Bassett Correctional Center
P.O. Box 11492
Oklahoma City 73136-0497
(405) 425-2900

Oregon

Michael McGee, Superintendent
Kevin Hormann, A and D Coordinator
Barbara Mealey, Program Services Manager
Julie Garvin, Education Manager
Columbia River Correctional Institution
9111 N.E. Sunderland Ave.
Portland 97211-1708
(503) 280-6646
FAX: (503) 280-6012

Sonia E. Hoyt, Superintendent
Oregon Women's Correctional Center
2809 State St.
Salem 97310-0500
(503) 373-1907

Pennsylvania

William J. Wolfe, Superintendent
State Correctional Institution at Cambridge Springs
451 Fullerton Avenue
Cambridge Springs 16403-1238
(814) 398-5400
FAX: (814) 398-5413

Mary Leftridge Byrd, Superintendent
Melinda A. Yowell, Parenting Program Director
State Correctional Institution at Muncy
P.O. Box 180
Muncy 17756
(717) 546-3171

Rhode Island

Roberta Richman, Warden
Alberta Baccari, Parenting Coordinator
Phone (401) 464-2366
Women's Division
P.O. Box 8312
Cranston 02920
(401) 464-2361
FAX: (401) 464-1842

South Carolina

E. Richard Bazzle, Warden
Florence Mauney, Deputy Warden for Programs
Leath Correctional Institution–Women
2809 Airport Rd
Greenwood 29649
(803) 229-5709
FAX: (803) 734-1293

Mary B. Scott, Warden
Synaya R. Jones, Administrative Assistant
Phone (803) 863-1337
Women's Correctional Center
4444 Broad River Rd
P.O. Box 21787
Columbia 29211-1787
(803) 896-8590
FAX: (803) 896-1226

South Dakota

James P. Smith, Warden
Dallas Schneider, Unit Manager
Springfield State Prison
Box 322
Springfield 57062-0322
(605) 369-2201
FAX: (605) 369-2813

Tennessee

John Patterson, Warden
Holly Metcalf, Administrative Assistant
Chattanooga Community Service Center
815 N. Hickory St.
Chattanooga 37404
(615) 634-3189
FAX: (615) 622-1606

Texas

Scott Comstock, Warden
Ernest Gremillion, Assistant Warden
Lockhart Correctional Facility
P.O. Box 1170
Lockhart 78644-1170
(512) 398-3480
FAX: (512) 398-4551

Utah

Jim Smith, Warden
Utah State Prison Olympus Facility
and Women's Pre-Release Facility
P.O. Box 250
Draper 84020
(801) 576-7000

Dr. Christine Mitchell
Director, Planning and Research
Utah Department of Corrections
6100 S. 300 E.
Salt Lake City 84107
(801) 265-5597

Vermont

John B. Murphy, Superintendent
Chittenden Regional Correctional Facility
Swift & Farrell Sts.
South Burlington 05403
(802) 863-7356
FAX: (802) 863-7473

Virginia

Wendy Hobbs, Warden
Virginia Correctional Center for Women
Box 1
Goochland 23063
(804) 784-3582

Washington

Alice Payne, Superintendent
Washington Corrections Center for Women
9601 Bujacich Rd. N.W.
P.O. Box 17
Gig Harbor 98335-0017
(206) 858-4200

West Virginia

Don Ervin, Administrator
Deborah M. Huck, Program Specialist
Charleston Work/Study Release Center
607 Brooks St.
Charleston 25301-1319
(304) 348-2763

Wisconsin

Kristine R. Krenke, Warden
Carole A. Pagel
Taycheedah Correctional Institution
N7139 County Highway K
Fond du Lac 54935-9099
(414) 929-3800
FAX: (414) 929-2946

Wyoming

Bruce Daniels, Warden
Alice Kern
Wyoming Women's Center
Box WWC20
Lusk 82225
(307) 334-3693

Federal Facilities

C. E. Floyd, Warden
Federal Satellite Camp
37900 N. 45 Ave., Department 1680
Phoenix, AZ 8502-77003
(602) 465-9757

Robert A. Hood, Warden
Federal Correctional Institution
8901 S. Wilmot Rd
Tucson, AZ 85706
(520) 574-7100

Loy S. Hayes, Warden
Federal Correctional Institution
Dublin
5701 8th St.
Camp Parks, CA 94568
(510) 833-7500

Charles Stewart, Jr., Warden
Maud MacArthur, Parenting Coordinator
Federal Correctional Institution
Rt 37
Danbury, CT 06811-3099
(203) 743-6471(x410)

Patricia Scholes, Corrections Specialist
National Institute of Corrections Information Center
1860 Industrial Circle, Suite A
Longmont, CO 80501
(800) 877-1461
FAX: (303) 682-0558

Sal Seanez, Warden
Federal Correctional Institution
3625 FCI Rd.
Marianna, FL 32446
(904) 526-2313
FAX: (904) 526-2788

David W. Helman, Warden
Federal Correctional Institution
P.O. Box 7000
Pekin, IL 6155-57000
(309) 346-8588

Harley G. Lappin, Warden
Federal Correctional Institution
Old Oxford Highway 75
Box 1000
Butner, NC 27509-1000
(919) 575-4541

Anne Beasley, Warden
James R. Schluter, Paralegal Specialist
Federal Prison Camp
1100 Ursuline St.
Drawer 2197
Bryan, TX 77805
(409) 823-1879
FAX: (409) 775-5681

William G. Saylor, Deputy Chief
Office of Research and Evaluation
Federal Bureau of Prisons
320 First Street, N.W.
Washington 20534
(202) 724-3121

Phillip S. Wise, Warden
Federal Prison Camp
Box B
Alderson WV 24910-0700
(304) 445-2901

Canada

Ontario

K. J. Wiseman, Assistant Commissioner
Communications and Executive Services
Correctional Service Canada
Sir Wilfred Laurier Building
340 Laurier Avenue W.
Ottawa, K1A 0P9
(613) 992-2973
FAX: (613) 995-3352

Mary Cassidy, Warden
Prison for Women
40 Sir John A. MacDonald Blvd.
P.O. Box 515
Kingston K7L 4W7
(613) 545-8531
FAX: (613) 545-8816

Manitoba
Wayne Bott, Superintendent
Portage Correctional Institution for Women
329 Duke Ave.
Portage La Prairie R1N 0S4
(204) 239-3389
FAX: (204) 239-3397

Newfoundland
Mary R. Ennis, Assistant Superintendent
Newfoundland and Labrador Correctional Centre for Women
646 Illinois Drive
P.O. Box 660
Stephenville A2N 3B5
(709) 643-5607

Quebec
Margaret Shaw, Professor
Concordia University
Montreal H4A 3M6
(514) 483-2808

Mexico
Lic. Luis Rivera Montes de Oca, Director General
Prevencion Y Readaptacion Social
Dr. Rio De La Loza No. 156
2o. Piso
Col. Doctores
Mexico, D.F. 06720

American Embassy
Arrest and Detentions Unit
Office of Citizens Consular Services (CCS)
Apartado Postal 88 Bis
Mexico City
Mexico I, D.F.

United Kingdom
Professor Sir Michael Rutter, FRS
MRC Child Psychiatry Unit
Institute of Psychiatry
University of London
De Crespigny Park, Denmark Hill London SE5 8AF
0171703 5411
FAX: 0171708 5800

Community Programs and Resources

American Bar Association Center on Children and the Law
Barbara E. Smith
1800 M St., NW
Washington, DC 20036
(202) 331-2649

Aid to Inmate Mothers (AIM), Inc.
Reneice Bellamy, Executive Director
P.O. Box 986
Montgomery, AL 361010986
(800) 679-0246

Angel Tree/Prison Fellowship Ministries
1856 Old Reston Ave.
Reston, VA 22090
(703) 478-0100

Dr. Adela Beckerman, Professor
Nova University
3301 College Avenue
Fort Lauderdale 33314
(800) 986-3223(x1447)
FAX: (305) 370-5698

Bedford Hills Correctional Facility/Children's Center
Catholic Charities
Sister Elaine Roulet, Director
247 Harris Rd.
Bedford Hills, NY 10507
(914) 241-3100 (x384)

Dr. James Boudouris, Consultant
Change and Evaluation, Inc.
617 44th Street
Des Moines 50312-2301
(515) 274-3205
E-mail : JBoudouris@aol.com

Center for Children of Incarcerated Parents
Denise Johnston, M.D., Director
714 West California Blvd.
Pasadena, CA 91105
(818) 397-1396

Centerforce, Inc.
Peter A. Breen, Director
64 Main St.
San Quentin, CA 94964
(415) 456-9980

CFAD (Continuite Famille Aupres
Des Detenues)
Yolande Trepanier, Director
661 Rose de Lima
Montreal, Quebec H4C 2L7
(514) 989-9891

Child and Family Policy Center, Inc., and
National Center for Service Integration
Charles Bruner, Director
1021 Fleming Building
218 6th Ave.
Des Moines, IA 50309
(512) 284-5047

John Rees, Vice President, Development
Corrections Corporation of America
102 Woodmont Blvd
Nashville, TN 37205
(615) 292-3100
FAX: (615) 269-8635

D.C. Family Literacy Project
Walter Hill, Director
1328 G Street, S.E.
Washington, DC 20003
(202) 673-7300

Dismas House of Owensboro
Gus Gesser, Director
530 Carlton Drive
Owensboro, KY 42303
(502) 685-6054
FAX: (502) 685-0081

Families in Crisis, Inc.
Susan Quinlan, Director
30 Arbor St.
Hartford, CT 06106
(203) 236-3593

Family & Corrections Network
Jim Mustin, Director
P.O. Box 244
Palmyra, VA 22963
(804) 589-3036

Family Focus Project
Rebecca Winslow, Contact Person
155 North First Avenue
Hillsboro, OR 97124-3072
(503) 693-4919

Family Works/The Osborne Association
Julie Broglin, Director
135 East 15th St.
New York, NY 10003
(212) 673-6633

Friends of Prisoners at Mitchellville
Rev. Carlos C. Jayne, Coordinator
800 E. 12th Street
Des Moines, IA 50316
(515) 262-2024

Friends Outside National Organization
Gretchen Newby, Contact Person
3031 Tisch Way, Suite 507
San Jose, CA 95128
(408) 985-8807

Girl Scouts Beyond Bars
National Institute of Justice
Marilyn Moses, Director
633 Indiana Ave., N.W. Room 805
Washington, DC 20531
(202) 514-6205

Grandparent Caregiver Advocacy Project (GCAP)
River Ginchild, Contact Person
100 McAllister Street
San Francisco, CA 94102
(415) 255-7036 (x321)

Dr. Alfred Healy, Professor of Pediatrics
University of Iowa Hospital School
Division of Developmental Disabilities
Iowa City, Iowa 52242
(319) 353-6390

Hope House
3789 Hoover St.
Redwood City, CA 94063
(415) 363-8735

Imprisoned Mothers Program
Edwin Gould Services for Children
Sister Mary Nearny
104 East 107th Street
New York, NY 10029
(212) 410-4200

Inmate Family Service, Inc.
Lufay Butler, Director
225 South Third St.
Philadelphia, PA 19106
(215) 351-1412

Justice Resource Centre/John Howard Society of Manitoba
Graham Reddoch, Director
583 Ellice Ave.
Winnipeg, Manitoba R3B 1Z7
(204) 775-1514

Justice Works Community
Shirley Cloyes, Executive Director
1012 Eighth Ave.
Brooklyn, NY 11215
(718) 499-6704
FAX: (718) 832-2832

Kids Need Moms, Inc.
Linda Shaffer, Coordinator
Marcia Nye, Volunteer Director
38 Fourth Street
Coldwater, MI 49036
(517) 2799165

The Las Comadres Program
Gretchen Newby, Director
P.O. Box 695
Chowchilla, CA 93610
(800) 748-5078

Legal Services for Prisoners with Children
Ellen Barry, Director
474 Valencia, Suite 230
San Francisco, CA 94103
(415) 255-7036

Men Inside Loving Kids (MILK)
Patricia B. Penn, Contact Person
P.O. Box 207C
Lawrenceville, VA 23868
(804) 848-4131

Mothers Inside Loving Kids (MILK)
Ginny Morton, CIRC, Contact Person
P.O. Box 1
Goochland, VA 28063
(804) 556-3321

National Commission on Correctional Health Care
Edward A. Harrison, President
2105 N. Southport
Chicago, IL 60614-4017
(312) 5280818
FAX: (312) 528-4915

National Criminal Justice Reference Service
Box 6000
Rockville, MD 20849-6000
(800) 851-3240

Jenni Gainsborough, Public Policy Coordinator
National Prison Project, ACLU Foundation
1875 Connecticut Ave. NW,#410
Washington 20009
(202) 234-4830
FAX:(202) 234-4890

Neil J. Houston House/Social Justice for Women
Phyllis Buccio Notaro, Contact Person
4 Notre Dame St.
Boston, MA 02119
(617) 482-0747

Linda Shafer, Coordinator
Marcie Nye, Volunteer Director
"Kids Need Moms" Program
Florence Crane Women's Facility
38 Fourth Street
Coldwater, MI 49036
(517) 279-9165

OPEN, Inc.
Ned Rollo, Consultant/Author
1308 Kynn Drive
Garland, TX 75041
(214) 271-1971

The Osborne Association
Elizabeth Gaynes, Executive Director
135 E. 15th Street
New York, NY 10003
(212) 673-6633

PACT, Inc./Support for Kids with Incarcerated Parents (SKIP)
Debra Key, Executive Director
2665 Gravel Dr.
Fort Worth, TX 76118
(817) 595-0995

Parent Resource Association
Ann Adalist Estrin, Director
213 Fernbrook Ave.
Wyncote, PA 19095
(215) 576-7961

Parents Anonymous
140 Clarendon St.
Boston, MA 02116
(617) 267-8077

Parents in Prison Advisory Board
Patricia Lockett
Department of Social Welfare
Tennessee State University
Nashville, TN 37209

Daniel Pollack, J. D., Professor
Wurzweiler School of Social Work
Yeshiva University
2495 Amsterdam Ave., Ste. 818
New York City, 10033-3299
(212) 960-0836

Presbyterian Criminal Justice Program of the Social Justice
100 Witherspoon St., Room 3044
Louisville, KY 40202

Prince William County Children's Support Groups
Maeve O'Neill, Contact Person
8033 Ashton Ave., Suite 107
Manassas, VA 22110
(703) 792-7783

Prison Family Foundation, Inc.
Daniel J. Bayse, Executive Director
643 Auburn Drive
Auburn, AL 36830
(334) 821-1150

Prison MATCH (Mothers And Their Children)
Rose Weilerstein
1080 Miller Avenue
Berkeley, CA 94708
(510) 524-3942

Prison MATCH of North Carolina, Inc.
Mabel Topping, Treasurer
63259 Falls of Neuse Road, #123
Raleigh, NC 27615
(919) 881-0797

Prison PATCH (Parents And Their Children)
June Pearse, Executive Director
P.O. Box 105454
Jefferson, MO 65110
(314) 751-4748 (x256)

Prison Playroom Project
Susanne Blough Abbott, Ed.D., Executive Director
18 Brantwood Lane
Stamford, CT 06903
(203) 322-3257

Prisoner Family Support
Jane Otte, Contact Person
P.O. Box 123
Marion, IL 62959
(618) 997-1227

Project HIP (Helping Incarcerated Parents)
Roberta Niehaus, Principal
117 Mallison Falls Road
Windham, ME 04062
(207) 892-6716

Project ImPACT/Peanut Butter & Jelly
Rachel Saiz, ImPACT Coordinator
1101 Lopez Southwest
Albuquerque, NM 87105
(505) 877-7060

Project SEEK (Services to Enable and Empower Kids)/Mott Health Center
Carol Burton Barnett, Contact Person
806 Tuuri Place
Flint, MI 48503
(313) 767-5750

Reconciliation Ministries
Karen Fletcher, Director
P.O. Box 90827
Nashville, TN 37209
(615) 292-6371

Right Turn, Inc.
152 Lynnway, Suite 1F
Lynn MA 01902
(617) 596-2224

Women's Prison Association and Hooper House
Ann L. Jacobs, Executive Director
110 Second Avenue
New York, NY 10003
(212) 674-1163